BEYOND DESERVING

BEYOND DESERVING

Children, Parents, and Responsibility Revisited

Dorothy W. Martyn

WILLIAM B. EERDMANS PUBLISHING COMPANY
GRAND RAPIDS, MICHIGAN / CAMBRIDGE, U.K.

For all the children

who have been my teachers

$Bl. Eerd. \ ^6/_{07} \ 14.00$

© 2007 Dorothy W. Martyn

Published 2007 by
Wm. B. Eerdmans Publishing Co.
2140 Oak Industrial Drive N.E., Grand Rapids, Michigan 49505 /
P.O. Box 163, Cambridge CB3 9PU U.K.

Printed in the United States of America

12 11 10 09 08 07   7 6 5 4 3 2 1

Library of Congress Cataloging-in-Publication Data

Martyn, Dorothy W.
    Beyond deserving: children, parents, and responsibility revisited / Dorothy W. Martyn.
        p.   cm.
    Includes bibliographical references.
    ISBN 978-0-8028-4422-4 (pbk.: alk. paper)
    1. Play therapy.   2. Child psychotherapy — Parent participation.
    3.   Poetry and children.   I. Title.
    [DNLM: 1. Play Therapy.   2. Child Psychology — methods.
    3. Parent-Child Relations.   4. Poetry.   5. Psychoanalytic Theory.
    WS 350.2 M388b   2007]
    RJ505.P6M363   2007
    618.92′891653 — dc22

                                                                2007003162

The author gratefully acknowledges permission to use extended quotations from copy-righted works granted by the publishers listed on page xii.

Contents

PREFACE   ix

ACKNOWLEDGMENTS   xi

Introduction   xiii
Context   xiii
The Thesis of the Book   xiv
The Structure of the Book   xvi
A Final Word   xxii

I. Three Children Show and Tell in Play Therapy

1. Anthony   3
Some Early Revelations of How Anthony Felt about Himself 3
Vignettes from School   4
*Landmarks of the Space Where Anthony Went When He
    "Spaced Out"*   5
*Star Wars: How Conflicts in Outer Space Speak to Those
    in the Inner Space*   8
Of Bubbles and Bottles; or, How Not to Wet the Bed   11
Focus on Three of Anthony's Most Difficult Tasks   13
On Taking Responsibility, or "Repairing the Landspeeder" 22

On Signs of Change: Reflections from "the Meridian"   23

2. Jennie   25

Vignettes of a Bright Blossom under a Cloud   25

In the Beginning: First Disclosures   26

Clues to Jennie's Inner Space   27

Jennie Wrestles with Her Conflicts   31

A Dog Changes His Spots   37

The Final House in the Playroom: A Houseboat Is
    Rigged for Sailing Off   38

3. Henry   40

A Creative Young Mind in Doubt   40

Prelude   41

Following the Leader   43

External Clues to Internal Challenges   44

Going Faster and Further and Hitting the Mark   50

Of War in the Fortress   51

Fish, Fishtraps, and "a Bird That Just Fits into Its Cage"   53

Viking Ships and Submarines   54

Henry Brings Us into Port   56

II. Seeing the Children's Presentations through Dickinson's Lens

4. The Family as the Main Garden   61

Family: Some Observations   61

What Does "Family" Mean Today?   63

The Central Hypothesis of This Book: Beyond Deserving   63

The Offense of This Radical Departure from a Basic
    Tenet of Social Living   64

The Qualities of Non-manipulative Love   68

Sources of Non-manipulative Love: Differing Conceptions   76

Contents

5. The "Minor" Role of the Garden Assistant   80

*Fi, fie, fo, fum! Is That Giant in the Attic after Me?
  Am I a Bad Parent?*   81

The Big Snag: "The past is never dead. It's not even past."   82

Bloom: What Would It Mean in Human Beings?   83

Love: Some Definitions   84

Work: That Other Aspect of Bloom   86

The Relationship between Love and Work   90

"Beyond Deserving" Assistance   92

6. The Major Actor: The Child   97

Packing the Bud: Stoking Future Potentialities   97

Opposing the Worm: Wrestling with Gnawing Conflicts   100

Obtaining the Right of Dew: Procuring Nourishment   104

Adjusting the Heat: Managing Anger and Sexual Strivings   108

Eluding the Wind: Coping with Internal and External Pressures   110

*Escaping the Prowling Bee: Contending with Overweening
  Conscience and "Meddling" Adults*   114

7. The Snake in the Garden   120

The Immortality of the Snake in the Garden   120

How Do We Recognize the Fellow?   121

Where Does the Snake Hide?   122

Severe Judgment Itself as the Culprit   123

The Bible as Witness?   125

Susie's Final Word to Us   126

Summing up Part II and Anticipating Part III   127

III. Remedies and Responsibility Revisited

8. Psychotherapy as a New Kind of Garden   131

What Is This "New Recipe" Called "Psychotherapy"?   132

Who Might Want It?   133

Its Form and Limits   133

Its Distinct Qualities   133

What Are the Dynamisms That Provide Its Potency?   134

A Strangely Powerful Dynamism: The Hidden Impulse to Repeat   135

A Second Powerful Dynamism in Psychotherapy: The Use of the Weapons of Self-Protection   145

The Third Powerful Dynamism: Dragons, Witches, Fairy Godmothers, and Gods — or, in Prose, "Transference"   148

9. Responsibility Revisited   152

Responsibility Has a History   152

Responsibility and the False Assumption of "Autonomy"   155

Making "Responsibility" More "Responsible"   156

Understanding and Knowing versus Simply "Doing Something": The Great Open Secret of Responsibility   159

Taking Responsibility for Our Ghosts   160

BIBLIOGRAPHY   162

INDEX   164

Preface

The seeds from which this book grew are many. In the words of one of the children you will meet shortly, there are, no doubt, "old-fashioned ghosts" in the genes of this work: my own mother's tender mercies; dim, early memories of being moved to tears by my father's preaching. "Education must begin with one's grandparents," I was told by an uncle, and so, no doubt, must books.

My first, highly gifted psychotherapeutic supervisor, Deborah Hample, overseeing the work of "Jennie" (Chapter 2), remarked that the child's acts and words in the play therapy room were "poetry." That comment took root in my mind and grew in its import as other children followed suit. In their poetic play imagery, they spontaneously unveiled what they could say in no other way about their deepest concerns, thereby confirming my mentor's brief utterance and planting an important seed.

Initially hearing of the poem about the blooming flower in a lecture on Emily Dickinson given by her definitive biographer, Richard Sewall, I saw in a lightning flash that the third stanza of the poem had a book hidden in it and that that book was, in fact, already growing in the therapeutic work of children placed in my care. The parallels between the tasks a flower has to carry out in order not to disappoint "Great Nature" and those that children must accomplish for the same reason were too compelling for a child therapist to resist.

The playroom odysseys presented in this book took place over many years, and in this kind of extended work, the gardener grows along with the flowers. As Professor Sewall said in one of his Dickinson lectures, "The poet does not just make the poem; the poem makes the poet." The same principle must be true for authors. I am an heir to great treasure through what was entrusted to me of the inner world of these children.

I can scarcely overstate the growing impact of the poetry of Emily Dickinson during the gestation years of this book. Her words constantly echoed what the children were expressing with a sharp resonance that continues to astonish me. I no longer can imagine life without this constant companion. Perhaps it is appropriate to let Dickinson speak for me at the outset:

> He ate and drank the precious Words —
> His Spirit grew robust —
> He knew no more that he was poor,
> Nor that his frame was Dust —
>
> He danced along the dingy Days
> And this Bequest of Wings
> Was but a Book — What Liberty
> A loosened spirit brings —

(#1587)

Acknowledgments

In the writing of this book, my indebtedness to others is "manifold," as the Psalmist might put it. I am grateful, not only to my parents, mentioned in the preface, but also to the teachers who taught me to hear and to love the great voices of our literary heritage and who persevered in conveying the art and discipline of writing, and to professors and psychoanalytic mentors who have left their indelible marks on my thinking and work. I name particularly Professor Ann Belford Ulanov and Professor Christopher Morse of Union Theological Seminary, and Dr. Henry Kellerman and Dr. Anthony Burry, through whose deep wells of psychoanalytic knowledge and expertise my own work as a psychotherapist has been nurtured.

I name also our three sons, Timothy, Peter, and David, under whose tutelage my husband and I had a second opportunity to grow up. They are major influences in what has been written here, and I express my gratitude to all of them.

I thank all the children who have been my teachers in the play therapy room, as well as their parents, who worked faithfully in harness with me in addressing their children's needs. I have learned from every patient who has given me the privilege of participating in his or her growth, and my gratitude goes to each of them.

The graciousness and generosity of William B. Eerdmans Jr. and of his staff, all of whom reflect that same spirit, are much appreciated. Among those, I want especially to thank Mary Hietbrink, whose sensitive, skilled, and non-intrusive editing has greatly enhanced the book, and Linda Bieze, who both initiated and contributed significantly to the final stages of the editing process, and thus assisted in bringing this ship from its long voyage at last into port.

There are several faithful friends who will not be named here (they will recognize themselves) who have supported, aided, and abetted this enterprise throughout. I am grateful to each of them.

I would also like to thank the courteous staff of Harvard University Press for their assistance in my being permitted to quote so liberally from the poems and letters of Emily Dickinson.

The help of my husband, J. Louis Martyn, is incalculable. Not only has he been a rock of support and encouragement from the beginning to the end, but his careful reading of the entire manuscript and his countless editorial improvements have greatly contributed to the final result. His exemplification, as spouse and parent, of the qualities of love that this book describes is a "word made flesh." Lastly, through more than five decades, his own profound theological work has infiltrated mine, thus helping to shape this book.

Excerpts from "Plant a Radish" from *The Fantasticks* are used by permission of Alfred Publishing Co., Inc. Lyrics by Harvey Schmidt; music by Tom Jones. Copyright © 1960, 1963 (renewed) by Tom Jones and Harvey Schmidt. Publication and allied rights assigned to Chappell & Co. All rights reserved.

Poems by Emily Dickinson reprinted by permission of the publishers and the Trustees of Amherst College from THE POEMS OF EMILY DICKINSON, Thomas H. Johnson, ed., Cambridge, Mass.: The Belknap Press of Harvard University Press, Copyright © 1951, 1955, 1979, 1983 by the President and Fellows of Harvard College.

Prose by Emily Dickinson reprinted by permission of the publishers of THE LETTERS OF EMILY DICKINSON, Thomas H. Johnson, ed., Cambridge, Mass.: The Belknap Press of Harvard University Press, Copyright © 1958, 1986, The President and Fellows of Harvard College; 1914, 1924, 1932, 1942 by Martha Dickinson Bianchi; 1952 by Alfred Leete Hampson; 1960 by Mary L. Hampson.

Introduction

Context

This book places itself within a recent trend toward a rapprochement between neuroscience and psychotherapy.

For at least two decades, research in the field of child development adopted almost exclusively a biological framework for understanding the working of children's minds. Issues of language and learning were focused on the physical brain. Important discoveries have been made about how neurological structures function and how chemical treatments can affect this functioning.

From antiquity, however, there has always been another approach, one which focuses on those elusive currents within and between human beings, emotions

> That Science cannot overtake
> But Human Nature feels.
>
> Emily Dickinson, #812

We have always had, and will surely continue to have, an ongoing debate between these two conceptions of mental health and mental illness and their implications for the rearing of children.

Currently, however, new evidence indicates that the two approaches, the biological and the psychotherapeutic, may be more compatible than previously thought. Indeed, Dr. Eric Kandell of Columbia University, primary author of the definitive text *Principles of Neural Science*, fourth edition (2000), and his colleagues at the Howard Hughes Medical Institute have been leaders in pioneering research that links the biological and the psychotherapeutic. They have, that is to say, verifiable evidence that *talk therapy* and *chemical treatments* have similar effects on certain portions of the brain. They made their work accessible to the public in a recent public television interview with journalist Charlie Rose (September, 2004).

This trend toward better relations between biology and the psychodynamic is also exemplified in *Descartes' Error: Emotion, Reason, and the Human Brain* by Antonio R. Damasio (Putnam, 1994). This eminent neurologist explores the close connection between the biology of human reason and the centrality of emotion in the very act of reasoning, further contributing to our understanding of the indivisibility of affective and cognitive functioning.

The Thesis of the Book

Drawing on twenty-five years of psychotherapeutic practice, I invite the reader to take an observer's chair in a play therapy room. In that setting, three children provide us with a special lens through which we may understand what goes on in their minds. The self-presentations of these young patients (anonymous, of course), in their original language, constitute the first third of the book, Part I.

My thesis grows out of the children's play therapy: a *beyond-deserving model* has true power to cultivate love and creative work in children, and, by extension, in all of us.

This phrase, "beyond deserving," may be a bit puzzling at first glance. After all, the idea of "deserving" permeates our language and is taken for granted in much of our daily life, from grades at school to rewards for exceptional performance — such as whether one "deserved" a gold medal or the Nobel Prize — to our ideas of criminal justice. "He got what he deserved," we might say about some poor wretch sentenced to execution for a foul crime, or about a child who received a humiliating failing grade in English for plagiarizing his term paper. Or, on the positive side, one might say to a friend, "A nice person like you deserves to have such a lovely necklace."

My own fascination with the truth that there is something very important beyond our deserving began some decades ago when I heard a sermon on the parable of the workers in the vineyard (Matt. 20:1-16), who all received the same pay from the master, though some had worked a long day, some a half-day, and some just a short part of a day.

The unforgettable gift from that sermon was a new understanding that the major biblical message is about something that cannot be earned. In this parable, "fairness" and "merit" utterly disappear in an in-breaking of a powerful force that transcends "deserving" altogether.

In my decades of working with children and families, the significance of this force has become incarnate before my eyes, as I have seen the superior potency of an approach to a "misbehaving" child that has no element of "this-for-that" implied in it. Thus gradually, over the years, there grew in my head the following discovery, which provides the fundamental thesis of the book:

Parental love, and, by extension, all mentoring love, is authentic and effectual in proportion to the degree that it transcends the commonly assumed principle of the circular exchange, that is to say, "this for that." All true love is a stranger to that kind of thinking. The "justice" idea of reward according to what is deserved is replaced by the much more powerful force of noncontingent, compassionate alliance with the essential personhood of the other, however small that part may appear to be, against the destructive forces opposing that person's good.

Part of what makes my thesis fly is what Keats called "the wings of poesy," that is, poetry, specifically from two sources:

- Poetry from children engaged in play therapy, who pour out their deepest concerns in a stream of creative imagery, which, like all art, gives expression to what cannot be uttered directly, and is therefore best described as "poetry."
- Poetry, secondarily, from a few of the great writers of our literary heritage, whose voices resonate with those of the children. In the meeting of young poets with older ones we find what William Faulkner, in his 1949 speech accepting the Nobel Prize for literature, called the only thing worth writing about: "the problems of the human heart in conflict with itself."

The origin of this thesis has a personal dimension. After studying theology, I was educated professionally in the field of psychology, drawing upon the knowledge of my mentors and colleagues in both disciplines. However, I have come to feel that it is from such disparate sources as the

Psalmist, and Shakespeare, and Isaiah, and Dickinson, and Wordsworth that we gain the deepest insights into these children. By extension, we can also understand better our own struggles between love and hate, between creative work and destructive impulses.

The Structure of the Book

Part I

Part I (Chapters 1-3) consists of three children's therapeutic journeys as they spontaneously unfolded in my play therapy room. In the context of a special relationship of deep trust, respect, and affection, the children's own imaginative productions, stories, and games reveal what was really troubling them. Equally important, when we learn to understand what children are saying through their own poetic language of play, we see that these productions themselves have healing power, for they enable the children to *address* their own conflicts and worries. Much of what is involved here is illuminated by a poem by Emily Dickinson that provides much of the structure and coherence for the entire book, for its reference to the flowering of plants is clearly an analogy to the flourishing of the human being in certain circumstances.

> Bloom — is Result — to meet a Flower
> And casually glance
> Would scarcely cause one to suspect
> The minor Circumstance
>
> Assisting in the Bright Affair
> So intricately done
> Then offered as a Butterfly
> To the Meridian —
>
> To pack the Bud — oppose the Worm —
> Obtain its right of Dew —
> Adjust the Heat — elude the Wind —
> Escape the prowling Bee

> Great Nature not to disappoint
> Awaiting Her that Day —
> To be a Flower, is profound
> Responsibility —
>
> Emily Dickinson, #1058

Of the many ways in which this poem can be read, one is as a comment on the kind of parenting that truly assists the gradual flourishing of a child. The poem is alluded to throughout this book in that light.

In play therapy that was based on the beyond deserving model, the three youngsters began to gain mastery over what was interfering with their own thriving. I have learned that the children's creations have as much power to heal as they have to reveal. What someone wisely said about poetry in general is altogether fitting in referring to these young creators: "The poet doesn't just make the poem; the poem makes the poet."

Part II

Part II (Chapters 4-7) uses Dickinson's poem as an interpretive framework for exploring yet more deeply what the children show us in their dramatic presentations.

Chapter 4: The Family as the Main Garden   After briefly focusing on the apparently changing nature of just what the "family" means in today's world, the chapter explores what is involved in a shift from a "this for that" model for parent and child to one in keeping with the book's thesis stated above, the superior potency of a different paradigm.

Particular qualities of genuine love are inherent in the "beyond deserving" model and constitute its special power. Fundamentally theological, these qualities can even be expressed in secular terms: (1) "Givenness," like the dew, just comes, unsummoned. It is itself a love that moves *first* and cannot be earned. (2) "Participation with" is a form of love that enters into the other's distress. This "withness," so different from "againstness," is the deep meaning of "mercy." (3) "Patience" is the kind of love that knows how to wait, how to accompany and sustain the child, allowing space and time for the other's own being to emerge without coercion.

Readers who are informed theologically will probably recognize that these "abstracted" ideas are drawn from the writings of Karl Barth. Indeed, everything that I have written since being struck by Barth's bolt of lightning has been fundamentally shaped by his biblical understanding of authentic love.

Here also I discuss a frequently encountered misunderstanding. Does not a departure from a "this for that" approach to child discipline imply a "permissive" stance toward child rearing? Emphatically no! On the contrary, the "beyond deserving" way is much more powerful in helping children with behavior than the older way of the circular exchange.

Chapter 4 ends with some thoughts about differing conceptions of the sources of this powerful kind of loving, as well as the role of poetry and other art in providing bridges between persons of quite different philosophic persuasions.

Chapter 5: The "Minor" Role of the Garden Assistant   The "minor Circumstance" of Dickinson's poem is the gardener — that is to say, the parents, teachers, and mentors who foster the growth of the child.

In my first close reading of this poem, I was surprised and puzzled by the phrase "The minor Circumstance/Assisting in the Bright Affair." In the transparent analogy being made between the plant world and the human world, could Dickinson possibly be suggesting that the gardener, the parent, is a "minor" part of the drama? Anyone who is, or has been, a parent has scarcely experienced the feeling of playing a "minor" role! The extent, the complexity, the unremitting hour-to-hour, day-to-day, year-to-year responsibility of the care of the young is a daunting undertaking, even under ideal circumstances. When complicating factors such as illness — physical or mental — financial reverses, serious conflict between the parents, or other unfortunate winds of circumstance beat down upon a home, the care of the young becomes truly formidable.

Making the parenting task still more demanding are the ghosts from the past that forever intrude on a new generation, bringing with them new versions of old wounds and unfinished emotional distress experienced in prior relationships, especially those with one's own parents. "The past is never dead," William Faulkner wrote. "It's not even past."[1] This is a truth

---

1. From REQUIEM FOR A NUN by William Faulkner; Ruth Ford, adapter; copyright 1950, 1951 by William Faulkner. Copyright 1959 by William Faulkner and Ruth Ford. Used by permission of Random House, Inc. (New York: Vintage, 1975), p. 80.

that often operates outside the field of awareness, but it is nevertheless a central factor in bringing up our young. It can bring great blessing when the past is full of love and cherishing, and great woe when the past is filled with pain and trauma. How can Dickinson say, in the face of all this complexity, that the parenting task is "minor Circumstance"?

She can make that assertion because the "profound Responsibility" for becoming a flower lies dominantly in the flower itself. That is to say, just as the gardener does not make the flower happen, so the parent does not make the child happen. A dynamic, internal design in both plants and children will unfold according to its own latent plan if the gardeners and adults involved are able to *assist* in the flowering, as distinguished from attempting to control or coerce the process of growing. "Assisting" in the context of a beyond-deserving model is here explicated with specific examples of interventions that are far more potent than "this for that." The difference between an "assisting" model and a permissive one is clarified in this way.

The "Bloom" in human beings lies in the growth of the ability to love and to work, and the chapter gives attention to the deeper meanings of those terms, as well as to the relationship between the two.

Chapter 6: The Major Actor: The Child   Here I address, one at a time, each of the intriguing metaphors presented in Dickinson's poem, showing how richly they symbolize the tasks children (and all of us) must accomplish in order to grow into mature human beings. What must flowers and children actually do? In order to grow and "become," they must

- pack the bud (stoke future potentialities)
- oppose the worm (wrestle with gnawing conflicts)
- obtain the right of dew (procure nourishment)
- adjust the heat (of anger and of sexual strivings)
- elude the wind (of inner and outer pressures)
- escape the prowling bee (of overweening conscience and what the child experiences as unneeded intrusion by parents)

Chapter 7: The Snake in the Garden   Here I draw upon the most famous crime and punishment story of our culture, that of the Garden of Eden, to shed light on my earlier assertion that every family is inevitably beset with some version of a "marplot" in their midst, that is, something that mars the plot. (I am indebted to Herman Melville for this useful word.) Our forebears referred to this unwanted reality as "original sin." Whatever we call it, there seems to be an ongoing condition that prevents every generation from starting over in virgin soil. There is always some inheritance, for better and for worse, from ancestors who are vanished but who are still here with us. The freight of this chapter has to do with "the worse" part of the inheritance.

One face of "the devil" is nothing other than severe judgment itself, especially as it becomes the self-accusatory, self-destructive voice of overweening conscience. I refer, then, to the children's compelling dramatizations of inner torment suffered under the persecuting judge within. One striking example of the demonic, sadistic power of this "devil" can be found in the story of "Susie" in Chapter 4. The terrible plight of her night terrors — her self-accusing tormentors — was discussed there in the context of the "mercy" brought to her by her parents' faithfulness in being *with* her rather than *against* her.

Chapter 7 ends by summarizing the role of parents and mentors as the "minor Circumstance" and by emphasizing the child as the major actor in the drama. By identifying the "Snake in the Garden" as severe, accusatory judgment of the self, we are now prepared to consider the notion that psychotherapy is a new kind of garden for some of those who have been deprived of dew, beset by devils of self-accusation, or troubled by heat they can't manage to adjust.

Part III

Part III (Chapters 8-9) explores remedies for children and revisits children's own responsibilities.

Chapter 8: Psychotherapy as a New Kind of Garden   In this chapter I bear my witness to a process to which I am personally deeply indebted, and through which I believe I have been able to be a

> "minor Circumstance
> Assisting in the Bright Affair"

of enhancing for some people their ability to struggle better with adverse winds, inner distress, and troubles with relationships.

The theory, or school of thought, on which my own understanding of effective psychotherapy rests is clearly Freudian, for that is the kind of therapy from which I myself profited, and it is the kind that I have practiced and have found to be useful for my patients. Explaining in some detail a complex process in non-technical language has been my goal in this chapter.

I am aware that some have a negative reaction to the word "psychotherapy" on the grounds that it supposedly discourages the "taking of responsibility" for one's own difficulties and problems in living. But here our instructors are Anthony, Jennie, and Henry.

In their journeys in play therapy, they were precisely "taking responsibility." It is easier to see that reality in children's work, perhaps because the young are so guileless and, through their poetic imagery, so transparent in their self-revelation. The unconscious mind has not yet managed to construct such high walls around itself to keep its secrets in the dark. We certainly noted their allusions to hiding and burying things underground and, indeed, to building fences in order "to keep out the ones we don't like" (Jennie). However, children do not yet have a cast-iron cover over their inner world, and that fact makes that inner world more accessible. The next and last chapter explores in more detail just what it was they were taking responsibility for.

Chapter 9: Responsibility Revisited   Revisiting here the children's material from the first three chapters, we see to what lengths they went to address their own difficulties. As Anthony said, "I have to find a way to get out of this mess."

At the same time, all three children were deeply aware that the responsibility for their difficulties did not lie with themselves alone. They sensed that antecedents for their problems had been provided by "scary and old-fashioned ghosts" (Jennie) and "icebergs that had been there for thousands of years and [were] impossible to thaw out" (Anthony). Those profound insights were, of course, unconscious and could be referred to only by the "poetry" of their play.

The weight of this chapter lies in its emphasis, following the example of the children, on taking responsibility for our "ghosts." We are more responsible, not less so, when we are aware of forces that are working on us beyond our ability to control them. These hidden forces are in all of us, and denial of that truth, along with actions that do not take that truth into account, is the height of irresponsibility.

To address forces not visible to the naked eye, both in ourselves and in others, is indeed the essence of responsibility, as it takes into account our limited autonomy. To believe that we can be "accountable" on the strength of what we consciously can know and do by the action of the will, without a high respect for what may be operating in us outside our awareness, is sheer folly. History is strewn with the wreckage left by heads of government who were unconscious of the infantile wish for power that resided in them, as it does in all of us, although it is largely hidden from our view.

One of the great open secrets about responsibility has to do, then, with understanding and knowing our subterranean selves versus simply "doing something." "Doing something" is what enables us to keep unconscious what is subterranean, thereby evading the responsibility to allow the discernment and judgment of the conscious mind to be brought to bear on our actions. The substitution of an act for knowing something or feeling something is the undoing of all responsibility. This final chapter brings us to the end of Dickinson's poem with new insight given us by the children's

> . . . Bright Affair
> So intricately done
>
>   . . .
>
> Great Nature not to disappoint
> Awaiting Her that Day —
> To be a Flower, is profound
> Responsibility —

A Final Word

This book is based on "the Love that moves the Sun and the other stars," to borrow the last words from Dante's great *Divine Comedy*. It is about deepening our understanding of the qualities of that greatest force in the world, the love that moves first toward us, the love that informs the effective nurturing of our children.

I. Three Children Show and Tell in Play Therapy

1. Anthony

Some Early Revelations of How Anthony Felt about Himself

"This airplane is no good," said this child, showing the shiny new toy to the play therapist. "The landing gear is always down. It doesn't have enough fuel, and it has a big oil leak." The plane could "fly a little if it starts on a cliff," he said, as he began to think out loud about whether there was some way to give it a boost so that it might go higher.

He put the plane down suddenly and made a picture of a large gun and lots of explosives. As he began to play with a toy cannon, he remarked that it was possible for a cannon to have trouble with aim, "but," he said with perhaps excessive emphasis, "it's not trouble for **me**." However, the cannon did seem to give him some difficulty, and he remarked repeatedly, "The ball comes out too soon."

Anthony, six and a half years old, launched a twenty-three-month period of once-weekly therapy sessions with these forthright communications about how he was feeling about himself, feelings he carefully concealed from himself in his remarks about the airplane and the cannon and in his drawing of the picture.

On the very first day, he seemed to be telling me that he intended to dive right into this new situation. At least that is the message I heard when, after looking briefly around the room, he thoughtfully began to construct a pond from play dough, and a toy frog nearby jumped right into the pond. He also seemed to warn me, however, to be careful not to intrude: He spoke of "keeping the windows dark, so people can't see in" and of "[keeping] people out."

3

Vignettes from School

By way of introduction, let me say a little about how I came to know Anthony in the first place, which may shed some light on why his airplane was having so much trouble getting off the ground, what in his life was misfiring, like the cannon, and what underlay the explosives in his picture. Or, in the terms of Dickinson's poem, what worms was he opposing, what heat was he adjusting, what winds eluding, what bees escaping, and what kind of dew was he looking for?

This bright, handsome first-grader was brought to me by his parents because they were noticing that he was fearful and unconfident, in need of a great deal of attention at home, hesitant in reaching out to friends, and not doing well in school. He was also still wetting the bed at night, and both they and he were worried about that problem.

Indeed, Anthony was beginning to have a rough time at school. As the teachers described it, and as test results indicated, he was having trouble in "the area of auditory attention, as well as difficulty with visual clues and details." He was having trouble concentrating, and the ability to sustain an effort was weak. He was deficient in immediate recall, "which involves mental alertness and the ability to suspend *irrelevant thought* [emphasis mine] while attending to the task at hand" — a novel way, it might seem, to describe a child's attending to the most relevant matters of his life from his point of view. However, these important matters constitute our entire subject matter, and we will return to them shortly.

Noting Anthony's superior ability in abstract reasoning, vocabulary, social judgment, information-processing, and problem-solving, teachers were puzzled and concerned about his poor progress in reading, following directions, and visual memory. There were reports that he seemed to "daydream" a great deal. His concerned instructors were suggesting to his parents various exercises in recall and concentration that, hopefully, would address his attention deficits.

Did you ever wonder what a child is daydreaming about when he can't concentrate on his work? Have you wondered what space it is that children go to when they "space out"?

Anthony was very generous with the geography of this space during his two-year course of therapy. In the vignettes from his first therapeutic session he has already given us an introduction to the subject; now he is going to tell us more.

Landmarks of the Space Where Anthony Went When He "Spaced Out"

Carrying Monsters Uphill: Troublesome Feelings?

The task of growing up seems inevitably to involve, from time to time, carrying heavy loads on the mind. Anthony put his rendition of this earthly freight very succinctly: "Got to carry that monster up the cliff." Then, after thought, he added, "Pull him up that cliff? Only a giant could do that."

Apparently the weight upon him seemed very heavy indeed. What was Anthony's great burden, preoccupying him at the expense of being able to do his work at school, play happily at home, and sleep without interruption at night?

Prehistoric Animals: Old Powerful Forces?

Like most children, Anthony found in dinosaurs a rich resource for alluding to his own wished-for size and power, as well as vehicles for giving vent to some of his own aggressive strivings. During one of our sessions he told me this story, in which he drew on some elements from *Star Wars:* "There are three people and a landspeeder and a dinosaur that likes to eat people, bones, and Kennel Ration dog food. His teeth are so sharp, they go 'Crunch, crunch.' They have cavities and no fillings big enough for them." At this point the young protagonist burped audibly and announced, "That's a dinosaur after eating bones." As the dinosaur reached for another bite, he said, "The dinosaur can't bite the landspeeder, so he goes to get his little brother." As the aggression in this scene went over the top — with dinosaurs throwing harpoons at the brother and Artoo Detoo, an important Star Wars figure that seemed here to stand in for Anthony, getting shot at by the cannon — Anthony said, "The clouds get burned up," and then "The dinosaur sneezes and blows out the fuse."

From this rich bit of drama, it is clear that for Anthony dinosaurs also represented dangerous forces threatening him, some ancient and unyielding power of a primitive nature. "It would take a long time," he said, "to teach the dinosaurs to let the riders ride on their backs." About the dinosaur's tail, he commented, "The skin and bony structure are so strong that no laser can penetrate it." Another time he told me, "I forgot to tell you about the — he's about to step on me — Ah, the dinosaur missed me."

Feeling Lost

At times Anthony expressed his distress in terms of being lost. "How could one dinosaur lose himself?" he mused aloud one day. "I guess he stuck himself into the ground with his horns." Early on he began to spell out the theme of being lost and then found, first by hiding marbles and asking me to find them, and then for weeks hiding himself and asking me to find him.

The experience of repeatedly being found seemed to him to be part of the "rescue" he was appealing for. This play of hiding and finding, which a child invariably hits upon early in life, may express his concern with the permanence of people close and important to him when they are absent. Could Anthony have been addressing with marbles the same issue that Freud's grandson addressed in the famous foundational text for all play therapy, when the child would make his toy disappear, saying, "Fort" ["Gone"], and then retrieve it, saying, "Da!" ["There!"], in the interest of mastering his feelings when his mother went away?

Or perhaps it was Anthony's yearning to be found himself that he was enacting here — his wish to be seen, to be heard, to be recognized.

Wrong Keys, Missing Missiles, and Locked Wings

Anthony's doubts about his own adequacy, already introduced above, began to run through his play like a theme in a symphony. The key to the handcuffs was the "wrong key," he said, and the key was "upside down." The rubber knife needed a thicker handle. There were missing missiles on the airplane, and the wings seemed to stay in the locked position. There seemed to be a constant concern about the relative sizes of things: Were the battleship guns large enough? The Lego set needed to be bigger. Shogun's gun seemed too small: "There should be a bigger one," he said.

The matter of perceived insufficiency of size was clearly troubling Anthony, and equipment seemed to be generally subject to malfunction: "The wires are not working," he said of one toy. He also made a number of

Star Wars–related comments. "The droids are all out of order"; "There is a pipe broken on the droid"; "Artoo Detoo can't move." The droids became very concerned about Luke Skywalker, because "the bloodstream going to his legs doesn't work." Anthony also remarked, "I don't know what's gone wrong with this rocket ship" and "The escape hatch has run out of fuel." He once said, supposedly of an overheated rocket ship, but really of himself, "It needs a rescue. . . ." Not a teddy bear; not a can opener; not a fork; "it needs a parachute."

All of these images of power and perceived loss of power alluded to the same preoccupation heralded by that airplane that had trouble getting off the ground and maintaining suitable altitude. From the beginning Anthony was telling us that he felt there was something wrong with him. Maybe a worm that will make itself better known as we proceed was eating at him, and he was engaging much of his waking energy in opposing that worm.

Let us look at some of the ways that Anthony spontaneously expressed his opposition to what was gnawing at him, preventing his attention to other important matters.

Unruly Cars and Wild Indians

In the very first session I had with Anthony, cars were running over people and bumping into each other, and one car pushed a horse right into the quicksand. Something was out of control, and the consequences were clearly serious. Those cars were behaving very aggressively, and the result was that someone's means of power and transport was sinking into oblivion.

By the second session, the cowboys and Indians had found their weapons and were after each other, and it was by no means certain who was going to get the upper hand. Indeed, in the very first battle, the Indians were winning. Anthony explained why: "The Indians have the horse this time, and they are all over the place." Also, they were hiding, and the horse was hiding, so they "couldn't be seen"; they "just faded into the wall." At the end there were three Indians and two cowboys, then two Indians and no cowboys. In Anthony's view, the Indians were "bad guys." Most young children, oblivious of certain social issues, use this imagery to represent their own aggressive impulses.

Here Anthony's play suggests that the bad guys had the advantage:

they had the power; they were numerous and ubiquitous; and they were invisible. Anthony's perceptions give us a pretty good idea of how he sized up his ability to command his own impulses in light of their strength, especially when he couldn't always see where they were hiding.

Cowboys and Indians are time-honored characters that children use to represent the inner war between their own impulses and their need to control these impulses, presumably because of the way our culture has represented cowboys as heroes and American Indians as a primitive and aggressive people. Anthony deployed them from time to time to represent his inner struggles, but he also had access to other casts of characters who could play the roles with equal aptness.

Star Wars: How Conflicts in Outer Space
Speak to Those in the Inner Space

The early eighties, when this child was enacting his epic poem, was the great heyday of space discoveries and children's fantasies about them. The toy manufacturers, in addition to the timeless soldiers and sailors and superheroes, provided a plethora of little figures from the wars in the stars. Like thousands of other children, Anthony found in these outer-space figures a wealth of ways to spell out the wars in his inner space — or, to use Dickinson's terms, to spell out what he had to obtain, oppose, adjust, elude, and escape.

Bad Guys, Good Guys, and a Friend

The adventures of Artoo Detoo and Luke Skywalker, the two heroes that Anthony seemed to use most often to represent himself, included an elaborate cast of characters. The most important of these was Darth Vader, the embodiment of evil. For weeks, with all of the graphic brutality of Homer's *Iliad*, the intense fight between the adversaries occupied center stage.

The weekly battlefront was replete with time bombs, deadly traps, shots fired at the hero's feet, rockets on fire, equipment failures, and an authoritative meddler who chased the good guys into a bottomless pit.

At a particularly dangerous point in the action, when the "commander's plan" was for Artoo Detoo to go into the cannon and shoot himself out of it, "He was so afraid they'd get him, he got into a tension cell." These life-threatening enemies were primarily parts of Anthony himself, and that "tension cell" was exactly where he was when he couldn't concentrate on his schoolwork.

In the end, the enemies were cast into bottomless craters and the black hole — a hard-won victory of the good over the bad. "That was ten years ago," Anthony explained, "and Darth Vader hasn't reached the bottom yet. But if you listen carefully, you will hear 'Splat!'"

In fact, "Splat" became the title of a story "written, produced, and directed by Anthony F." At his request I audiotaped the tale over a period of three sessions. His own commentary on his fascinating story was, "Boy, I bet that guy has a headache. I better buy some Bayer aspirin."

An Ally

One among hundreds of interesting details in the epic of the star wars was the way in which Anthony employed, or deployed, the medical droid.

The medical droid was the transparent representative of the therapist, this new "listening person" in his life whom he had sensed from the first to be a friend: "Then there was a new team, and the good guys won the second round because of a "better plan." Most of the time Anthony saw the medical droid as a benign and helpful figure: "The medical droid had so many arms you could rest on them. . . . They would make a bed that could hold you up." Once, when the heroes and their enemies were found to be in a death-like struggle (the "Splat" saga), Anthony described the medical droid as having a bottle of "Splat" in each of his many arms to throw at the enemy.

From time to time Anthony found different ways to visualize his connection to this figure. Once he extended a string from a beleaguered ship and literally tied it to the medical droid. He often saw this figure as a powerful ally: "These people have to get the medical droid on their side to win the war." At one point he explained, "A person that used magic brought them [the creatures that had been turned to stone] back to life." Present here was a mere "assistant" that Anthony saw as a kind of magician.

However, this character was by no means always seen in a positive light. Once Anthony had his hero say, "You meddling droid! I'll put you under." Another time, when I had missed an important communication from him, he said, "The medical droid has to have its head examined. Its brain is made of Styrofoam!" At one juncture in our work together, when Anthony's father was quite unhappy with me, I was put on notice about the seriousness of the situation when the hero in the game announced, "Jabba [the Hut] is angry and is going to kill the medical droid."

The ordeals of the hero in all these deadly battles give us some idea of the desperate urgency Anthony was feeling about the powerful enemies he was experiencing from without and within himself. We can now see why studying phonetics and numbers paled in the face of what he was wrestling with. It is because children desire "to be good" — that is, to win out over "the bad guys" — that these matters can take such precedence over the more mundane demands of the classroom.

Searching for Control

Every child wants to have the upper hand over his destructive impulses, though this desire is not always obvious to adults when the child's impulsive urges win out. Much of Anthony's play with the heroes and their adversaries had to do with the arduous task of bringing the destructive aggressive urges to heel.

One time he told me, "Everybody's working on the control, because it really got shot up. . . . Everybody is working on the control tower because the enemy [the dinosaur monster] is hiding behind the microphone." Another time, when his hero was being pursued by a bad guy, a giant put a knife into the monster and turned him to stone. When Darth Vader had been threatening his hero with some terrible fate, the hero fought valiantly and finally was victorious: "This is the moment I've long been waiting for — to take the saber of Darth Vader: I have him weaponless."

One factor made the control problem even more complicated. "The Indians win and the cowboys are dead," Anthony explained once, because of a "surprise attack." At another point he said, "They're in there just having a good time and don't know there's going to be an attack." He also lets us know how such a thing could happen: "It was a great time for a surprise attack because everyone was busy."

These remarks give us an idea of how difficult it is for a child to attend to all his battle stations at once. In other words, he can be caught off guard when his mind is occupied by a feeling or an urge that comes up quickly. Another young man once described this difficulty when he was explaining the role of a soldier he provided with a cushion to fall on. "You see," he told me, "he must not land too hard or too quickly." When I invited him to say more, he said, "These are the guys who give the other guys the signal when something is about to happen." This was a child who had enormous difficulty controlling his sudden aggressive upsurges, and through his play he was finding a way to get more warning time.

Of Bubbles and Bottles; or, How Not to Wet the Bed

One of the indications of the difficulty Anthony was having with the conflict between his urges and their control was the complaint that he was frequently wetting his bed. Apparently the strong currents of feeling that he could not easily deal with in his waking life found involuntary expression in the night. He himself started to speak overtly of this problem one day. In the middle of playing, he suddenly blurted out, "I am a bed-wetter, uh-uh . . ." Then he quickly reverted to a symbolic way of dealing with the issue.

He had thought of an ingenious way to symbolize the struggle to keep the feelings — and the urine — from leaking out by using a bottle of bubbles. In an early session, he had picked up the bottle, opened it, and quickly closed it again. A few minutes later he went back to the bottle and began to blow bubbles around the room. Suddenly it became very important to him to have his mother watch the bubble game, so he ran to the waiting room to fetch her. He wanted to show her that he could "keep the bubbles from hitting the ground." Later, he made it clearer what was at stake here when he attempted, repeatedly, to catch the bubbles and put them back into the bottle. Anthony frequently repeated this sequence of play, and slowly a mysterious change began to take place: the symptom of bed-wetting began to wane. If we assume that this development had to do with a shift in his feelings, we need to ask what they were about.

To focus more sharply on this question, let us pause briefly to assess where we have been and where we are going in terms of Dickinson's guiding poem (offered in full in the introduction) about how flowers "bloom."

In the sections above, we can notice how much of Anthony's play has had to do with "adjusting the heat" — that is, his attempting to address some of his angry feelings, which stemmed at least partially from the frustration of his wishes for more warmth and more "dew." We might say that he was hot from anger about the feelings of chill, or the low settings of the emotional thermostat in the family. As I noted earlier, he once spoke about bringing creatures back to life "that had turned to stone."

Anthony also told me a story about an underground base "sixteen miles from the North Pole" where there were "tunnels made of ice." He spoke of "icebergs that had been there for thousands of years" and were impossible to thaw out. In addition, he drew a picture about "a space war among four planets." (Where else might we find four parties in troubled interaction?) He depicted "an Ice Raider" that interfered with the power line between cold little Pluto and the distant Sun. When I asked about Pluto's predicament, Anthony replied, "It's important because Pluto has to get his power from the Sun." Since a boy derives his sense of forcefulness primarily from his father, and since this boy had a father who might have seemed emotionally distant, we could make an educated guess here about the identity of the Sun in his picture.

The play that Anthony called "Splat" is full of references to angry feelings. In one scene he spoke of "flaming wires — all burning, and fire so hot it could turn the ice red." Also, the missiles "burn up the clouds, and then it's very cold." In drawing a picture of exploding fireworks, he referred to the discomfort of being too close to them. "If I stood here," he said, holding a felt pen up in the air, "I could be above the fireworks."

We can guess that fear as well as anger were among the strong feelings that were causing Anthony so much distress, but, when we review what he revealed to us, we see that the anger predominated. This was evident in a dinosaur scenario he described to me: "These guys [dinosaurs] are mad! Even though they were plant-eaters, they bit each other on the neck, and they both died."

In another scene, Anthony described how the hero Shogun, in the heat of a battle, "goes to a big oil tank and throws a match in and blows the world into smithereens." Even though, in terms of this particular drama, it is Shogun who does this infamous deed, we can guess whose anger is being reflected here. When I expressed interest in the reason for Shogun's act, Anthony replied as though responding to a matter of fact: "He's programmed to do it."

These vignettes make it clear why Anthony found "adjusting the heat" such a formidable task. He was angry about the matters he revealed. This anger, which always seeks a target, was at least partially directed at his parents over the frustration of his wish for more supplies for his emotional hunger and thirst and for more warmth in the family.

None of this means that his parents were "at fault." They were doing the very best they could for their boys with the supplies they had been given. But they were wise to seek help with what they felt they had been unable to give.

The difficulty was that the parents had also grown up in chilly families, where feelings could not be easily expressed and wishes for more nurturance were not fulfillable. Like their son, they themselves felt they were not powerful enough to do what was important to do. I will say more about these fears of inadequacy in the following section.

Focus on Three of Anthony's Most Difficult Tasks

Opposing the Worm: Oedipus "Wrecks,"
or What Was Gnawing on the Vitals

Among those engaging metaphors that Dickinson employs in her poem to liken the tasks of the flower to those of a human creature, none is more suggestive than that worm. Would there be a more apt way to describe what all of us experience in wrestling with "the human heart in conflict with itself"?

All of the feelings described in the above sections gave Anthony some trouble, and the struggles would be a part of the "worm" he had to oppose. But there is more to the story.

Anthony's most distracting conflict had to do with the great open secret known from antiquity, enunciated by the Greeks, resonant through the literature of all cultures, and close to the center of every child's emotional freight: the fear of a child having to do with the rivalry with one of his parents. Herein lies a tale so significant and so mysterious and so weighty that we will devote several pages to Anthony's rendition of it.

This timeless, predictable, inevitable, and apparently indispensable drama is yet to be absent from any course of play therapy I have ever participated in — that is, the struggle that ensues from the child's secret, unconscious wishes to displace the parent of the same sex and to enjoy the spoils of priority in the affections of the other parent.

The crisis that this rivalry brings about is an enormous challenge for all children. However, handling the complexities of this thorny matter seems to contribute to the mature formation of personality and constitutes a necessary part of a child's emotional preparation for a satisfying emotional life with a later partner.

The primeval wish to overcome one's parent and even unconsciously to wish this parent dead and gone in the interest of procuring the other parent for oneself brings with it enormous dangers in the child's mind. To wish ardently for a treasure that rightfully belongs to someone else is to bring on oneself the deep fear of the retribution that would seem appropriate to the crime. Children always have an instinctive understanding that possessing the position of priority with mother or father does not rightfully belong to them, and that therefore their wishes, if fulfilled, involve not only stealing but also what amounts to murder.

A part of the seriousness of the matter for children is the degree to which they are still subject to magical thinking, especially the thought that the wish is the same as the deed. Children suffer powerful unconscious feelings of remorse as a result of these wishes for the unattainable: that one parent could be utterly eliminated so that they could have all the treasure for themselves. As Anthony put it during one of his battle scenes, "'Cause each wanted to be the only survivor — special, and better than the others."

In addition, the primitive moral sense that children have not yet refined — witness their resonance with the extreme retributive "justice" of fairy tales — requires "an eye for an eye and a tooth for a tooth." Their own unconscious impulses to possess the longed-for but illicit treasure of preeminence with the adored parent are matched in intensity by a profound fear of retribution in kind. If one wishes one's mother or father dead, then one deserves to be punished, even unto death. Such fear would shed light on a vociferous protest Anthony once made in the middle of a game of "Clue," when we were both trying to solve the mystery of a crime. Anthony said suddenly, "I'm not the murderer!"

There is something about this timeless drama that we do not want to believe and that keeps slipping out of the awareness of parents and educators. We do not seem to like this ancient story, and we keep pretending that it is not true, even though it resounds through the literature of all cultures and all ages and lives in the heart of every child. Sophocles' *Oedipus Rex* and Shakespeare's *Macbeth*, as examples, may seem to be stuffy old outmoded dramas that have nothing to do with modern life, but have you ever felt the collective pulse of an audience when some hero or heroine is caught in a similar triangular crisis? Did you ever see the film *The Great Train Robbery?* Did you catch the nearly intolerable suspense of the audience when the thief was about to succeed in getting the gold on the moving train? The gasps of fright as he was apprehended? The enormous relief when, at the clever ending, chicken feathers covered the entire screen, and it would never be clear whether or not the thief was caught?

Steinbeck once said that "a story lives when it tells us about ourselves." For some reason, the infinitely varying but never changing renditions of this story never die, and they never cease to engage us. Fairy tales, movies, computer games, opera, and soap opera, as well as great works of literary genius — all sound the same theme that pervaded Anthony's drama. His version was written with toys and paint and creative imagination in a small playroom under the interested and nonjudgmental eye of a caring adult serving as an assistant.

It may be that all of the metaphors in Dickinson's poem come into play when a child wrestles through this inevitable childhood struggle. The energy to "pack the bud," or stoke one's potentialities for the future, is certainly deeply affected by this developmental hurdle. Much adjustment of the heat is also involved, in regard to both the strength of the passionate wishes that are stirred and the anger at the frustration of those wishes.

Anthony's brilliant, transparent, and, in the end, efficacious rendition of these important matters will, I believe, sway the skeptics who like to dismiss them as simply "Freudian." Here is Anthony's own presentation of many of the "irrelevant thought processes" that were interfering with his work — namely, the occupation of his mind with this fantasied battle for the position of king of the mountain.

One day, a little over a year into his work, Anthony introduced the idea of a bank robber who found himself in jail. In this version, rather than casting the drama with small toys, Anthony elected to play all the parts himself. He began this particular play with the robber trying to reach the keys to the jail (the prop of a box of actual keys being set near to hand). The robber did manage to reach the keys, but he was caught by the guard when he tried to escape and was put back in jail. The guard handcuffed the robber's hands behind his back, and he put the keys even farther away. Because the jail was put on wheels, the robber managed to reach the faraway keys. But the guard caught him again, and this time put chains on the key box. However, when the guard went out to lunch, the robber got loose from the handcuffs, successfully robbed the bank, and still had plenty of time to escape.

About three weeks after introducing this venturesome situation, Anthony re-introduced the robber theme. Again he was the robber in the play. He was in jail, but the door was left open. He put the handcuffs in front of him, broke the chains, and got the box of keys. He was rejailed several times, and the task of escaping became harder and harder, and the robberies and ensuing shootouts with police got repeated over and over. The desperate scene escalated into the criminal's being imprisoned in the mayor's office and finding the mayor's keys in a drawer — but alas, they didn't work on the handcuffs. After long thought, Anthony in his role of robber rolled the mayor's chair (my office chair, which he had co-opted for this important enterprise) over to a bookshelf, selected a book, and started to "read." When I expressed interest in why he was reading, he said, "I have to find out how to get out of this mess."

He then narrated a sequence of events. First, he turned the chair over and broke the chains of the handcuffs. Then he threw a knife at the mayor's neck and killed him, and consequently was put back in jail. At the end of one such episode, the robber, in a futile attempt to escape, was shot dead by the mayor.

The details of the drama above shifted slightly from week to week, but essentially the plot was always the same: the robber was imprisoned, managed to escape, and was caught — and punished by the authorities. In one episode, the mayor found out that the culprit had his keys because the robber had left the keys in the wrong place. "I got caught going into the mayor's office and escaping," Anthony explained.

There were endlessly varied allusions to the running contest between the thief and the authorities and the lengths to which he had to go to try to escape the inexorable forces of retribution. "I thought I would have to cut myself to get loose," Anthony said during one rendition of the play, "but I've lost my knife." His variations were always specific and graphic. "This guy had to shrink his hand so the rifle wouldn't fall out." "Got a pistol because it is easier to hide." "I know a time bomb is ticking." "It is crazy to hold a time bomb in your hand that is about to go off." "I have to find the right key before it goes off." "The last word is going to be 'boom.'" "It went off and blew me up." "The only thing that could get me is electricity — the electric charge gets me." "They bring in more men. I kill them." "Seven years later they catch me." "I'm in jail for life, but I'm locking the police officers in their own jail. I kill them all." "They get more forces! All the army in the world! All I have is this dagger, and they have guns." "I'm surrounded." "I shoot the cops." "'If you shoot, I'll cut up the money.' The police die and I live."

The urge to rob and the consequences of that urge continued to escalate. Once, when there were 500 policemen in the bank, I asked Anthony, "How does that work out?" He said, "Easy — not rob it." In attempting to rob a spaceship, he successfully got the ship and tried to take it to "outer space." Again, Anthony used very graphic detail. "I'm at 12,000 feet and rising. I am going into hyperspace." "Only one trouble: this guy doesn't know how to drive rocketships." "Going much faster than I should be going; my speedometer cracks." "Going into black hole — the gobbling mouth of black hole." "Wanted to rob it and ended up going through the black hole."

Anthony vividly expressed the seriousness of his predicament in one of his renditions. "Open the vault," he yelled at me, then "Say you can't." I said what I was supposed to say, and then he stabbed me with the rubber knife. "Now I'm wanted for two crimes — for robbing a bank and killing somebody." After this criminal action, he created a "supersonic plastic jail." He described it as "harder to escape from than Alcatraz! Alcatraz is weak compared to this."

Successive versions of the drama seemed to increase both the extent of the spoils and the necessity for tighter and more secure restraints. After breaking out of the supersonic plastic jail, Anthony decided to rob the bank where the diamonds were kept, then demanded all the money in the world from the bank tellers "by sundown." When I, as a hapless bank teller, couldn't accede to his demand, he killed me over and over. Again, Anthony was very detailed in his story-telling. "He finds a jewel, the most valuable in the world . . . fifty billion jewels." "He robs the mine, the richest in the world." "So much money it is hard to carry; he bends under the load." "They were so dumb, they didn't tie my hands." "Now I have to take the jail with me." Grenades and volcanoes and repeated murders of me when I didn't come up with "all that's left of the world" culminated in his throwing a match in a big oil tank and "blowing the world into smithereens."

It seemed that he was at least as concerned about the ultimate incarceration as he was about the ultimate robbery. He invented a "jail inside a jail." "Five jails — inside one." "Too many — I can't do it." "Too crowded in there."

Once, when he found "his knife too short," he killed a policeman with a snake. A humorous "Pardon me" when he put dynamite in a monster's mouth scarcely altered the mounting intensity in the struggle. The "cops came into the robber's hideout," Anthony explained, "and spears fell from the roof that were going to hit the cops. Only one cop still alive. Took my knuckle chain, knocked the cop out from behind. Got caught again and was tied up with 10,000 burning hot tubes. A laser came flaming out, but I melted his gun." This apex of metaphor led him one day to another idea: "I'm going to hypnotize myself so I will never stop robbing banks." While making this pronouncement, he tied a stopwatch to his head and swung it back and forth as though to execute the hypnosis.

In one of Anthony's last renditions of his plight, when he was trying relentlessly "to get into a despicable vault," yelling "I can't get into it!", in his frustration he bent the rubber knife "into a question mark." "What is the question?" I asked. His answer: "Will I get into it? The world will never know."

Thus Anthony summed up the inevitable and apparently necessary plight in which children find themselves enmeshed: that of the desire somehow to possess and be the favored one with a loved parent whom they know to belong rightfully to someone else. Another six-year-old, in inventing his own version of the struggle, responded to my casual inquiry about the cause of the fracas between the bad guys and the good guys with, "Because the gold belongs to them, and the bad guys are trying to take it."

Eluding the Wind: Strong Drafts
That Touched Anthony through His Family

The wind in the metaphoric series is used here to refer to currents that blow, with varying intensity, on children from outside circumstances and especially through families. In Chapter 6 we will look more closely at this and the other metaphors borrowed from Dickinson's poem in regard to the tasks involved in growing up. For now, it is enough to point to a few of the winds that affected Anthony.

This child was keenly attuned to the insecurity his parents felt from time to time in regard to their own adequacy, their own health, and the viability of their business ventures. When parents are threatened, their children can feel hurricane-level winds that shake their own foundations.

One instance of such a fright for Anthony had to do with an unusual business reversal that hit his parents quite suddenly and severely, making them so anxious that their health was affected. His father became extremely anxious, and his mother began to experience an aggravation of a muscular disorder that was quite frightening to the entire family. At about this time, Anthony began to show signs of obvious emotional distress and regression in his bed-wetting. He cast the matter in two very revealing ways.

First he painted a striking picture of the crisis at home. There was "a war in outer space," he told me, and the fallout of "shrapnel" was causing both Pluto and Saturn (himself and his brother) "to be wiped." The picture had much fog, much anger, and many insurmountable obstacles. As he painted the picture, Anthony made a variety of vivid comments. "I want to come closer to it. It is very foggy." (He apparently had an urgent need to see what was going on in the family.) "There are billions of pieces of shrapnel. . . . The road is burning. . . ." (He made purple splotches in the picture.) "Purple flames make an obstacle course. . . . Very close to being blind because of the explosion. . . . Over here is thicker fog. . . . Almost pitch black. . . . Fog is important to keep you in the dark." It was also about to rain. And scientists found something humongous happening in space: there was a star hurtling toward the black hole. "The outer-space people were having a war."

An intriguing and revealing detail in the picture and its commentary was the discovery among the ruins in the scene of "a computer — many others too." Also, "trailers full of stuff were destroyed." These are transparent references to the failing product involved in the business distress that Anthony's parents were experiencing.

Then there was a long "ghost in the attic" story that Anthony dictated to me over three sessions. Much of the story was obscure to me, but there was one reference that could not be missed: There was a "dangerous metal thing . . . a powerful thing that could kill everybody. . . . It's like a computer. . . . There are computers everywhere." He drew a picture showing the world being rained on by computers.

The destruction was massive. "Fort Knox is leveled in flames — 75-foot flames," Anthony said. "That metal thing could be a deadly conclusion." Then he commented, "My brother doesn't like it either" — an unusual insertion of a very simple everyday statement into the middle of the fantasy. "The metal thing is so powerful, it can destroy five cities and seven states, everything between here and Fort Knox, Snocks, and Chicken Pox," he said, with an apparent attempt to ease his fright somewhat by closing

19

the story with a touch of humor. But this attempt was unsuccessful. For some weeks, Anthony's symptoms of daydreaming and bed-wetting intensified until his family finally found a way out of their predicament.

I mention this incident to illustrate the fact that children know what is going on and respond to the stresses their parents are feeling, even when parents make careful attempts not to discuss difficult matters in front of them. Anthony summarized his view of the business situation during the crisis by stating, in the context of his play, "These people did a crazy thing: they shot a net out over the hole and tried to cross over it. But the suction in the black hole was too strong, and they should have known it was too strong, and it broke the chain." Never underestimate the perspicacity of children.

Escaping the Prowling Bee: Some Stings from Invasive Parties Who Wanted Anthony to Produce

How can the bee give us another way of looking at what a flower, or a child, has to do in order "not to disappoint Great Nature"? Well, bees invade in the interest of productivity. They also sting, and we can use that idea too. Like the bees, adults who want to facilitate a child's productivity can seem very invasive to that child.

Anthony felt very keenly the pressures to produce. Not only did he feel that he had to be a superachiever, but he felt he had to do everything in record time. This pressure for speed kept him rushing through things pell-mell and detracted from the quality of his work.

One of the ways he spoke of the problem was in connection with the landing gear on his airplane. "If it comes out too fast, the flight is unstable, and it can't land properly. If it comes out too slow, it could crack. It has to be timed right. But it could be a little too slow or too fast, and it would be okay." While Anthony's statement suggests that he understood the matter very well, in actuality he was always trying to drive himself to greater and greater speed.

The suffering that Anthony endured over not finding himself "fast enough" found many expressions in our time together. Of a stopwatch, which he had requested, he said, "I'm glad it's not mine. Then I would have to go twice as fast." He also commented, "If you put down your gun for three seconds, it is gone." He addressed this issue of speed in many different ways, and he tried to get relief from it by becoming the one who required the speed instead of being the victim of it.

Frequently, he saw me as a sluggard, and he told me that I had to learn to do things faster. When he gave me a number fact, I should "get it instantly," he said. "You have two seconds. Time's up!" he would yell. One day he walked in and began the session by rushing me before anything at all had happened. He picked up a book, as though to give me my weekly "test," which he loved to do, and then said "Time's up!" even before issuing a question. In addition, he claimed that my tape recorder was not fast enough. "Even on fast forward, it isn't fast enough. My brother's tape recorder does a whole song in one second."

In addition to the buzzing that Anthony may have sensed as messages from teachers and parents to get his work done, a large part of this pressure he imposed on himself as he watched and compared himself to what he called the "landspeeding" pace of his older brother and his father. Indeed, when I risked asking him about where the need for so much speed had come from, he answered, "From my brother!"

His older brother was indeed exceedingly competent and, to Anthony's distress, exceedingly fast. But the brother was the secondary bee here; behind him was a bigger bee. The father was a successful businessman whose way of life was to let no grass grow under his feet. He was a gold-at-the-end-of-the-rainbow man, with the remarkable ability to climb right up the rainbow and to come back with the gold. (The failed business venture described above was a striking exception.)

His father's ability to achieve business success was both a blessing and a bane to Anthony. His father's achievement made it possible for the family to have their material needs readily and generously met and provided a certain security and an ambience of abundance. These were the positive effects.

But the negative effects of the father's "landspeeding" — successfully internalized and utilized by the older son — felt like a sting to Anthony, a sensitive, quiet, introspective little boy who was struggling to find his footing in such a fast-paced family. A large part of those flaming wires and burning knives and exploding fireworks that Anthony drew and described so vividly had to do with his feeling impinged upon by these felt expectations to produce according to the precedents set before him. He was not only angry about the external messages that he should produce but also fearful that he could not measure up to the expectations, which added fuel to the fire.

The fear gave him further difficulty because he felt it was unacceptable. Once, when his actors "had to go into an underground pipeline in order to steal oil," they found that the oil wells were dry, and "they had to go steal oil with burning knives." "Was that scary?" I asked. "Oh, no," he responded, "no more than if I just went outside." Then he said, "But even if they want to be scared, they can't, because they are programmed not to be scared." At other times he said, "I'm not built to feel any fear" and (of his actors) "They couldn't feel fright but could feel anger a hundred times more than real people." Apparently Anthony believed that both fear and anger had to be "buried underground," and we can speculate that both were finding expression in his bed-wetting.

The threat that comes from the possibility of being stung by a parental bee is amplified by the transformation of this external bee into an even more severe internal one, which is a necessary and troublesome part of growing up. This is an important issue that I will deal with in some depth in later chapters. I will show that the interior "Goblin Bee — that will not state — its sting" (Dickinson, #511) lies at the heart of the matter of interference in not disappointing "Great Nature."

On Taking Responsibility, or "Repairing the Landspeeder"

One day, toward the end of his second year in the playroom, Anthony announced that Luke Skywalker "was learning the Force himself." He began to talk about a lot of "repair work on the landspeeder." He "tuned" it, worked on the wheels of the droid, and put stronger magnets on the feet of his hero.

He also began making making pronouncements that suggested increasing capability. "The medical droid, . . . part a medical droid and part a fixing droid, . . . works on him." "Ben Kenobi finds footprints and finds the enemy." "The key box is right in my hand. . . . Nothing can stop me." "He's taking a lot more supplies and forces from the base than before." "He is programming the droids himself so they can work for him." Most strikingly, Anthony told me that Yoda was "teaching Luke the Force." He also commented, "I see Yawa's hand is too small — I have to make it a little bigger. I have to give him a different gun." Luke Skywalker also tried to find a way to make the runway longer. Anthony voiced out loud concern about work: "Are you too lazy to do your work? Just give me a missile that works!"

One of Anthony's heroes seemed to have discovered over time something that worked for him, as this character announced, "I can handle all the jobs now." When I wondered aloud one day how one of the characters was feeling, Anthony replied, with astonishing overtness, "How do I feel? I feel confident — I know exactly how to get out of this mess."

In his last session (about twenty-three months from the first session), Anthony read me a good-bye letter he had written. In it he remembered the days when he was "in the lowest reading group." After finishing the letter, he began to destroy the cliff that he had used to fly his plane from and said, "I used to think it had to take off from a high place. But it doesn't. The wind speed makes it go up . . . , [but] the only way to be sure is to destroy the cliff." Then he performed another intriguing action: he destroyed "all the defenders or the guardians of the dark crystal and the guardian of the jewel." But, he explained to me, "it is not the end of them — they're going to the bottomless pit. Maybe they are trying to level into dust now." (This statement was one of the closest allusions to burying — repressing — I have heard from a child.)

This relegation to the depths of something that had preoccupied Anthony so long — this business of contests for jewels — was somehow being laid to rest, though a part of him knew that it was, as Faulkner put it, "vanished but not gone."[1] The conflicting forces can be handled in such a way that they are rendered less harmful, as Anthony has shown us, and ameliorated sufficiently for the practical matter of getting on with living.

Anthony's final words to his droids were, "Keep on drinking your oil."

On Signs of Change: Reflections from "the Meridian"

About a year after Anthony began his epic poem, there began to emerge external confirmation of improvement in the picture. When he completed second grade, a report indicated that the school, where his private work in the playroom was never known, was "pleased with his progress." The child who had needed drill in recall and attention scored, for example, in the

1. From GO DOWN, MOSES, by William Faulkner, copyright 1940 by William Faulkner and renewed 1968 by Estelle Faulkner and Jill Faulkner Summers. Used by permission of Random House, Inc. (New York: Random House, 1973).

93rd percentile on standardized tests in mathematics, and the concern that he was unable to concentrate on his work had disappeared.

Was this child who worked so avidly and tirelessly in the playroom on the interferences in his work the same child who "couldn't focus and concentrate his efforts," the same child who was having difficulty with "symbol relationships" and needed "specific exercises to address attention deficits"? The paradox here is that the key to the academic difficulties lay in the apparently "irrelevant thought processes" themselves. Far from being irrelevant, the distracting thoughts contained the ore for the missing power. "Where danger lies," said the poet Hölderlin, "grows the saving also."[2]

Anthony's play therapy, along with the weekly guidance sessions for his parents, which enabled them to understand and provide more fully the dew he needed, did over a period of two years result in making significant inroads into his emotional distress and thus the interference in his learning and work.

To sum up in the images of Dickinson's poem, Anthony had learned better to "pack his bud" in terms of stoking his future potentialities; to "oppose the worm" — that is, the worrisome inner conflicts that were distracting him and eating up important resources; to "obtain his right of dew" — that is, to procure for himself the necessary supplies for his self-esteem and potency; and to "adjust the heat" so that he no longer had to sustain and repress an overload of fear and anger. He had also built better fences with which to "elude the wind" and feel stronger in the presence of "prowling bees."

2. F. Hölderlin, "Patmos," in Friedrich Hölderlin, *Werke,* Gedichte 6. Available on the Internet.

2. Jennie

Vignettes of a Bright Blossom under a Cloud

A bright flower appeared in my playroom one day in the form of a lovely eight-year-old girl with a very appealing presence. She told me in various ways that things were gnawing at her, that there were scary things she wanted to elude and escape. And, over time, she allowed me to assist in adjusting the considerable heat that she was feeling in connection with these threats. The dreams that she was eager to tell me about described these matters vividly:

> "My face was invisible. I had to wear a mask. Then they finally found out I had a mask. Then my face came back."
>
> "I was being chased by a monster. . . . There were roots of a big tree all over the ground, and I kept tripping and falling. I had to keep getting up and running around."
>
> "There was a big dog; it kept jumping and jumping on me."

These dream images prompted many questions. Why did she find it necessary to wear a mask? What monster was chasing her, what big animal did she have to fend off? What was it that she kept tripping over, and why did she have to stay in motion?

Like Anthony, Jennie quickly found ways in the play-therapy ambience to express her own questions, and over a period of two years there emerged an epic drama through which she revealed how she took responsibility for her part in not "disappointing Great Nature."

In the Beginning: First Disclosures

Precisely because Jennie found it necessary to "wear a mask," the adults in her life, her parents and teachers, had a limited view of her inner distress. This engaging young girl gave her parents reason for only mild concern. To be sure, they thought she was overly conscientious, inordinately anxious to please, and perfectionistic in her standards for herself. Worrying about what people might think of her, she was quite fearful of making any mistake, had difficulty with attention to detail, and sometimes was "blocked" in mathematics. Any sign of conflict in the family sent her running in tears to her room. Easily frustrated, she tended to isolate herself at times and to withdraw into books a great deal. Her teacher described her as "wistful and dreamy," and her parents found her more fearful of physical dangers than would seem warranted by her situation in the real world. She seemed overly solicitous of her little sister. Sometimes she wet her bed.

Jennie was in many ways a model child. Notwithstanding the observations above, she excelled in her schoolwork and delighted her parents and teachers with her thoughtfulness and her exemplary conduct. However, something betrayed the presence of inner difficulty in a way that troubled the benign surface: she developed a nervous habit of clearing her throat frequently for no apparent reason. When someone called this matter to her attention, she gave up the habit and replaced it with a tic: she began to blink her eyes repeatedly, as though holding something back — some feeling? or perhaps tears? What was revealed as she commenced play therapy?

In her first session Jennie laboriously brought forth a picture of a glittering star. At her next visit, the star herself appeared in a dazzling performance. She arrived with a carefully prepared agenda for the session. "I wrote it all down for you," she explained, "but I forgot to bring it. But I know it anyway." Jennie then presented me with the most astonishing array of entertainment, which she had carefully prepared: riddles, jokes, stories, some facts she had learned in science class, three dreams, and some other memorized bits that sufficed to fill the hour. She was understandably exhausted at the end of this spectacular display, which she had planned and executed, no doubt, to please this latest adult in her life and to excel in the newly assigned task of psychotherapy.

The following week, reaching tentatively toward the toys in the playroom, Jennie sketched out a battlefield in the sandbox between soldiers in red uniforms and soldiers in blue uniforms. The distribution of power between the two sides — between the reds and the blues — appeared to be a matter of concern to her. She counted and recounted the numbers of horses and men on both sides and considered thoughtfully whether an advantage of more space for the blue soldiers would help to make up for fewer horses and men. She assigned and reassigned and then assigned again the horses and guns. She mentioned that there were not enough riders for the horses and also began to look around for fences, "to keep out the ones we don't like." She did not reach a satisfactory solution for herself about the relative power of the opposing forces and seemed to leave that question open. The only hint she gave about the nature of the conflict was this: "The Americans are very angry with the British because of all the bad things the British did."

What do we observe in Jennie's play? The lens we will be using to see it better is, again, the poem by Dickinson that is quoted in full in the introduction. While we will be looking more closely at the poem later on, for now we will use the allusion in the third stanza to "opposing the worm." We sense that in her play, Jennie had already begun to give live form to something that was gnawing at her. In this vignette she told us that there was a conflict between certain forces, that there was uncertainty about the relative strength of these forces, that there might not be, in her view, adequate control and direction for some of the power, and that there was a need to erect barriers against unwelcome parties. She thus alluded to the possibility of prowling intruders that she wanted protection from and to other dangers that she was somehow aware of. She also revealed that someone was angry at an overlord and that there were "bad things" at the root of the anger.

Clues to Jennie's Inner Space

Jennie Makes a House

One day, after thinking in silence for some time, Jennie turned to a large pad of paper and announced that she was going to make a picture. Tentatively at first, with pencil lines barely visible on the paper, she began to draw some lines and finally said, "It's going to be a house." Beginning with what amounted to a floor plan, Jennie used some heavy paper and Scotch tape and erected, over a period of some weeks, a remarkable paper dwelling, complete with carefully planned and constructed paper furniture in each room.

In the course of the work, Jennie stated pictorially a number of matters that were on her mind. In rendering a facsimile of a bedroom with a double bed, she struggled with the inadequacy of the original sketch to accommodate the furniture and, after much erasure and uncertainty, ended by enlarging the walls, quite literally, to alleviate the apparently crowded condition there. In the bathroom, she measured and remeasured the fixtures and, after a week's interval, measured again. She stated emphatically that the toilet was too small and proceeded to make a larger one, after which she again checked its proportions relative to the other furniture in the house. "That's better," she said.

The question arises, Why did she need a larger facility for elimination? What did she need to get rid of for which she felt there was insufficient means of discharge?

She also wrestled with another disproportion. She had begun to devise a playroom in her house, but on second thought decided it should be a workroom, with appropriate appurtenances for study. She assembled a gigantic bookshelf that towered over the entire house like a colossus. After loading it down with minute paper books, she considered the piece for a while and then said, "I like it, but I think it is too tall, don't you?" and proceeded immediately to correct its dimensions relative to the rest of the building.

Further elaborations of the scene introduced other questions. A tree began to grow at one corner of the yard, wrought with paper, crayons, Scotch tape, and much perseverance. It seemed that the height and erectness of that tree were of paramount importance to Jennie, as she worked week after week to remedy its tendency to droop. One day I mentioned that it seemed important to her that the tree stand up straight and tall. "Yes," she replied, "it has to be strong because I'm trying to put a kid in the swing." What, or who, stood behind this image of a tree that had to be sturdy enough to support the free movement of a child?

Jennie's ingenuity in giving vivid symbolic representation to inner concerns gave rise one day to a large red doghouse far removed from the house proper. In fact, Jennie placed the doghouse in the most remote corner of the yard. It seemed that certain inhabitants of her world were not welcome in her main residence; they needed to be isolated. Could it be that certain parts of herself needed to be kept separate from the rest of her? Did this structure have some reference, perhaps, to the same theme as the big dog in her dreams, that dog that repeatedly jumped on her? And did the red color of the house suggest what might be sheltered there? Did the red mean "red hot"? Did it refer to certain fiery feelings such as anger or sexual feelings? Is Dickinson's "adjusting the heat" a way of interpreting what was developing in this truly creative drama?

In fact, Jennie was introducing us to where she went when, as her teachers said, she "spaced out." This "wistful and dreamy" girl was anything but inactive. She was energetically finding new ways to struggle with the forces that underlay her troubling symptoms: the nervous tics, the bedwetting, and the emotional withdrawal. She was actually building a new house inside herself.

Stirrings in the House: People, Caterpillars, Mice, Worms, and Other Visitors

At last people arrived in the house. A mother paper doll, tall and thin like Jennie's own mother, found her abode there, along with a little girl with long blonde hair like Jennie's. A father doll came too, but Jennie changed her mind about him and recast him as a "baby brother," perhaps solving with this revision two problems for herself. Could it be that she was condensing into one small, non-threatening sibling the more complex and thorny relationships with both her father and her little sister?

With a family now inhabiting the house, other signs of life became evident. Jennie came to her session one day accompanied by two live caterpillars in a covered jar. "Their names are Harry and Beggar, and they are going to live in the doghouse," she announced. She proceeded, with the help of a stick, to communicate this plan to the caterpillars. These wriggly little creatures did not appear to be enthusiastic about their new residence, and it required repeated efforts by two of the paper dolls, the mother and the little girl, to corral them into the doghouse. In the course of the hour the beasties came at last under satisfactory control of their owners, who, with the help of two pencils, gained considerable expertise in their management. Once the caterpillars were tamed a bit, they were allowed to play on the swing, which now hung triumphantly from the tall paper tree.

Since both the child paper doll and the mother paper doll seemed to

be involved in this tricky enterprise of getting the elusive creatures to behave, I risked the question, "Who can manage Harry and Beggar — the
mother or the little girl?" "They both can," Jennie replied after some
thought.

We can probably assume that these little beasts, allowed to play and
swing under the watchful eye of their keepers, represented vital impulses
deep within Jennie that had been relegated to isolation. Now they were beginning to come forth in her own play sphere. When she reported sadly the
following week the untimely death of Harry and Beggar, she added a
thought-provoking comment. She sighed and said, "It would have been
nice if they could have become butterflies." In fact, that sigh revealed a fer-
vent hope expressed in her next move.

The vital stirrings represented by the caterpillars did not depart; they
found new embodiments. They reappeared one day in a drawing of several
little mice playing on the grass. Two were playing ball; some were picnick-
ing; one was riding a bike. "There are going to be others," Jennie said.
These mice, playing and basking under a bright yellow sun, seemed, like
the caterpillars, to be giving life to something previously buried that was
now allowed to play a little.

Other images took up this theme. Arriving one day with a troubled
look, Jennie began her session by saying, "I wanted to show you something, but . . . look." Unfolding her tightly clasped hand, she displayed a little crumpled heap of green thread. "It was a worm," she explained, "but he
wasn't very strong. He only cost ten cents, and I didn't take very good care
of him. But I wanted you to see him. He was so nice." I encouraged her to
talk about the disappointment and asked her what the worm might have
done if he could have survived to come to the playroom. She replied, "Oh,
he could sail through the air, and dance, and fly around. He could do all
sorts of things. But I knew he wasn't very strong; I should have put him in
his little case before I put him in my pocket."

The following week she came happily with another string worm, this
one only moderately deteriorated, having been better protected. "I'll show
you," she announced, "what all he can do." Then began a kind of "dance of
the worm." With the help of an invisible thread, he flew through the air.
Holding her fingers up, Jennie demonstrated the worm's agility in going in
and out and through her fingers. He danced in and out of the toy stove,
under the chair, and frolicked in great freedom around the entire room.

Jennie's joy in the dancing worm was palpable, and when this worm met the fate of his predecessor, she was saddened and thoughtful. "I know," she said. "I will make him a coffin." With loving care and much patience, she molded a clay coffin, carefully lining it with black satin and embellishing it with red felt. "The lid must have a handle," she decided. Before the little worm in its coffin was interred in a bottom drawer, she had made sure, by gluing a handle on the lid, that some access to what was represented there was indeed secured.

It can scarcely escape our notice that Jennie was trying to gain mastery over impulse in such a way that she could experience its animation and vitality without throttling its force and power. It is one of the most difficult tasks that children have to achieve: learning how to regulate impulse without killing it. It would indeed have been nice if the caterpillars could have become butterflies — and in fact, in her own case, as we shall see, they did!

Jennie Wrestles with Her Conflicts

Old-Fashioned Ghosts and Other Frightening Spectres

But other events preceded the above-mentioned transformation. Along with the relatively benign caterpillars, mice, and worms, other characters appeared that Jennie apparently felt to be less benign. Some "scary and old-fashioned ghosts" came to haunt the playroom for a while in the form of some handkerchief puppets that Jennie herself made. They seemed to suggest that some very old feelings were beginning to make their appearance in her present-day world. An alligator with fierce, sharp teeth sounded the theme of aggression in a series of paintings and drawings that Jennie did following the arrival of the old-fashioned ghosts. A huge red monster loomed over an entire sheet of drawing paper, with the dubious caption, "I luv you." A snake, bulging with recently swallowed prey, crept onto the paper and elicited this comment from Jennie: "It's a bad snake; it could kill us, you know."

A little girl with flaming red cheeks and an enormous mouth that seemed ready to bite nails appeared in another picture. Once loosened, angry and explosive feelings came roaring out in some visual word pictures, illustrating "Bang!" and "Rip!" with brilliant fireworks on display. Recalling again Dickinson's poem, we can see that in Jennie's case there was considerable heat to be adjusted, and that had to be done by Jennie herself.

She accomplished this in her play therapy by bringing the heat to the surface in order to harness it for her own use.

Jennie made various attempts to come to terms with these overly hot feelings in her paintings. She experimented with multilayered pictures, such as a red monster sketched out with crayons and covered over heavily with black, then etched with fine stylus lines to let a hint of the red show through. She designed in both paper and clay a series of monster cartoons in which she seemed to pursue mastery over these feelings through the time-honored method of humor. Some of these monsters were distinctly female, with long earrings and fancy headdresses. One was a spider, which Jennie tamed with a lovely hat with colorful flowers, addressing, perhaps, a long-standing fear of literal spiders, but also of some figure or force that the spider represented.

In some pictures, Jennie experimented with totally good feelings. In one drawing, dolphins, "which are friendly and let you ride on them sometimes," inhabited a sunny, pleasant harbor. In a succeeding version, however, one of the dolphins found himself jumping through red hoops, as though it might be a good idea to put some restraint on this playful fellow.

Jennie had not made final peace with her aggressive feelings. As one of her miniature figures put it one day, "I still feel like an Indian." As objectionable as this formulation is to our modern ear, it is true that children in our society still use this image to refer to aggressive impulses, partly, perhaps, because their parents still watch the old movies in which Native Americans are habitually cast in the role of fearsome aggressor. Though not politically correct, Jennie's comment was certainly emotionally correct.

The Search for Freedom in Containment

What could be done about the aggressive impulses themselves? Jennie cast around for some solution to this problem. Perhaps a container tighter than a doghouse. Perhaps a jail would serve the purpose?

Some bank robbers entered the scene one day, only to find themselves immediately taken captive in a fight with some Lego policemen, who hauled the culprits off to a jail of wooden blocks. Jennie seemed dissatisfied with this solution, however, and, after some thought, she began to build a "deeper place," as she put it, "where bad guys go when they are *really* bad." This deeper place was concretely established by a revised architecture: more blocks were called into service, and a two-level jail replaced the one-level kind. The offenders who were "really bad" could now be assigned to the more secure facility of the lower floor. Was Jennie alluding inadvertently to her unconscious mind, a building with a lower basement floor, where the "really bad" feelings could be housed out of sight?

Further action on the security front took place in this same session by means of small cars in the sandbox. A speeding vehicle encountered a police car, and both vehicles disappeared under the sand. "I like it better covered up with sand," Jennie said simply. Then a bus went out of control, tearing around the sandbox, literally raising dust and leaving a scene of destruction in its path. With the help of the police car and a tow truck, she hauled the bus into a parking place and used some small rocks to anchor the wheels. She seemed satisfied with this solution of control over unruly forces, indicating that the rocks should certainly "hold him," since the wheels could now not move at all. When I asked her about this, Jennie revealed that "the bus was very angry and had to be stopped."

Not moving the wheels at all is, of course, an unsuccessful solution to the problem of impulse, and it is not uncommon for children to try out this very defense against troublesome feelings. "Lacks motivation," a prevalent educational lament on report cards, often conceals this very attempt to control feelings by "not moving the wheels at all." This way of handling impulse can plague a person right into adult life and interfere drastically with both work and love. As Dickinson reminds us,

. . . the Heart with the heaviest freight on —
Doesn't — always — move —

Dickinson, #688

From one perspective, Jennie's entire journey in the playroom could be viewed as a search for appropriate containment of her impulses, some means of housing vital energies without losing contact with them. She had begun depicting this search through her image of the doghouse and continued it by constructing the coffin for the little worm as well as the jail for the robbers. She now carried it further with a sequence of play with houses made of cards. She began to experiment one day with the playing cards, trying one way and then another to build four-walled structures with them. "They are for the animals," she explained. "Each animal is going to have its own house." However, the booths that Jennie made for the small plastic animals proved to be quite precarious. In addition, she objected to their closed-off effect. She tried leaving one side of the booths open, like doors, but they proved too fragile for entrance and egress of the animals. At the end of a discouraging hour spent in attempts to fortify the card structures, the house of cards came tumbling down. "Well," Jennie sighed, "it doesn't matter. Next time I'm going to build a stronger house."

The next week, the stronger house began to take shape, this time made with wooden blocks. Jennie assessed each animal as to size and provided each with a separate booth. "They are going to have doors this time, because I want to be able to reach them," she told me. "I want to play with them, you see."

Indeed, Jennie had some plans for these animals, plans that required accessibility. The cow, for example, came out of her house one day, walked up to the fence that surrounded the animal compound, and surveyed the land beyond the enclosure. "The cow," said Jennie, "likes to pretend she can't get out. You see, she used to be in captivity, and, while she likes being more free, sometimes she likes to remember what it was like when she was in captivity." The tiger had the duty of "watching for wild things," and the troublesome hippopotamus, who could not control his bicycle, had to be securely bound to his vehicle with rubber bands. Jennie's statements about these animals continued the theme of freedom: "These animals are very lucky," she commented. "They can do lots of things — not like the animals that are in captivity."

Jennie kept dramatizing the need for forms that could contain vital impulses while also allowing some freedom. One day, while she was telling me about some interesting things she was making at school in connection with a particular project, she took up some string and began idly to work with it. Soon she began to weave something out of the string, which turned out to be a sort of container. "It could hold something, I think," she said, as she began looking around the room for "something it could hold." The following session, she made a little paper box, made a sign reading "Jennie," and put the sign in the box. Later on, she picked up the box, mused about it, and said, "It's too small; we need a bigger one." Cleverly manipulating paper, scissors, and tape, she produced a larger version and attached a sign that read "The Big Box."

The Big Box stayed on the table, and each week Jennie put things inside it. She made a tiny jack-in-the-box, considered it, and said, "It doesn't work very well." She then made another, more tightly constructed one, pronounced it good, and placed it inside the Big Box. A small stuffed bird accompanied Jennie to her session one day, and he too went into the box. Jennie looked troubled, however, as she put the bird in the box and announced, "I'm going to do something I've been thinking about for a long time." Then she took the bird from the Big Box and moved to a table where she liked to work with clay. She began to construct something from the clay after carefully measuring the bird with her hand. She began by saying, "You know, I really don't know what this is going to be." However, by the end of two sessions of tenacious effort, she had produced, to her moderate satisfaction, a kind of airy, grill-work structure that she announced was a "cage" for the bird.

When Jennie arrived the following week to find that the cage had collapsed, she was discouraged but not defeated. "I know what I will do," she said, and, within the hour, she had made a handsomely constructed and sturdy birdbath, firmly reinforced by some wooden sticks. She retrieved the bird from its collapsed cage, and, with an air of triumph, settled it snugly into its new abode, apparently quite pleased with her new creation. She had designed a living space for the bird — and the life force within herself represented by the bird — that offered some distinct advantages to both: the birdbath had a sturdy base; it was open to the air, providing freedom; and it had the added accommodation of life-giving water. The vital stirrings that we first saw in the wriggly caterpillars, the dancing worm, and the animals "out of captivity" had now found some acceptable containment, less radical than total enclosure and open to the freedom of sky and breeze.

Nobler Dwellings

A large, smiling snail crawled onto Jennie's drawing paper one day, and it kept reappearing in picture after picture. What might the spiraling chambers of this creature be representing to her? Jennie did not share her own thoughts with me. My own silent associations recalled part of the Oliver Wendell Holmes poem about the chambered nautilus that I had memorized in school:

> Build thee more stately mansions, O my soul,
> As the swift seasons roll!
> Leave thy low-vaulted past!

And, indeed, Jennie began to confirm that she was sounding the motif of enlarged boundaries. One day she brought with her a doll with a retinue of belongings: a suitcase, clothing for all occasions, a dog with two puppies, a mama horse and a baby horse, various pieces of toy furniture, and a hatbox stuffed with jewelry. "She's getting ready to move," she announced, "because her old house is too small and too crowded." Using the building blocks, she began construction on a new edifice, making numerous modifications and enlargements as the enterprise proceeded.

When Jennie was satisfied with the adequacy of the new house, she started to construct a station wagon, which grew and grew until she was sure it would "hold all the girl's things for moving." Then came the big moment. She piled all of the doll's possessions onto the station wagon and, with the excitement appropriate to such an important event, maneuvered all of the paraphernalia into the garage of the new house. Soon afterward, Jennie successfully installed the doll herself in the new dwelling, complete with a warm hearth provided by a clay fireplace and home-baked bread shaped carefully from play dough.

The House Within, as Represented
by the Dolls' Evolving Residence

For many months Jennie expressed through the life of this doll certain changes she felt were taking place within herself. She provided for all the needs of her heroine, who had found a yet stronger dwelling within a drawer, less subject to the exigencies of building blocks. She also brought a companion doll — "to be her friend" — and gave thought to the dolls' requirements. She gave them food for sumptuous dining; she frequently took them to the beach for pleasure outings; she arranged and rearranged their furniture, "in order to have more space." As their creator, she provided them with paper books made especially for them, and each week she gave them a new book, placed in their hands, to enjoy during her absence.

One day Jennie changed her mind about leaving books for the girls. "I think they should do something else," she said. "After all, they can't read all the time. I'm going to let them play with the animals instead." She was clearly referring to her own tendency to withdraw into books as a way of avoiding the risks of a fuller life; she was beginning to consider other options without abandoning her books.

As the weeks passed, Jennie's parents and teachers began to notice changes. Jennie's nervous tic — the involuntary, repetitive blinking — disappeared. Reports from school revealed a happier, friendlier little girl who no longer had spells of forgetting what she had wanted to say, and her problems in mathematics were a thing of the past. Jennie was able to express her feelings more openly; she could get angry when the occasion called for it; and she did not seem so fearful of physical dangers.

A Dog Changes His Spots

Jennie expressed the changes she sensed to be going on in herself by addressing, from time to time, her fantasy about one of her earlier creations, a clay version of her dog, Spot. She had used gray clay for the body of the dog and had superimposed white spots. She had been critical of the dog's appearance when she made him, and had said, "He sure is fat, and he's kind of ugly." Nevertheless, she had decided to keep the dog; she placed him in a drawer which, over the course of her working with me, became a museum of all her clay pieces. From time to time she removed the dog and mused about him, pondering his appearance, but she did not reveal her thoughts.

Many months later, she took the dog out of the drawer, looked at him, and said to me, "You know, I'm not sure this is the way Spot really is. I'm not sure whether he is black with white spots or white with black spots. Sometimes he looks one way, and sometimes he looks the other way. If you look at him from one direction, maybe he's black with white spots, and from the other direction, he's white with black spots. Hmm." Later still, she considered the question once more and said, "You know, I'm pretty sure Spot is white with black spots, and not black with white spots." She then proceeded to make a new version of the dog, reversing the proportion of black to white. When she considered the two models side by side, she announced, "I like the new one better." This revision would seem to tell us something about how Jennie felt about herself at the beginning of the work and how, over the course of time, she changed this perception. Something shifty, "fat," and "ugly" had yielded to something more acceptable in her mind's eye, and in her self-image.

The Final House in the Playroom:
A Houseboat Is Rigged for Sailing Off

On a day in early spring of Jennie's second year in the playroom, she told her mother, "I think when I have finished fifth grade, I will not be coming here anymore." It was clear to her, to her parents, and to me that her play therapy, as a particular kind of enlargement of her boundaries, had nearly reached completion. She no longer felt so much pressure to wear a mask. The monster that kept chasing her — the bad feelings within, which had kept her on such a treadmill of attempted perfection — had been partially tamed, and she discovered that her own impulses could be controlled in less rigid containers. The deeply buried roots that kept tripping her up — the unconscious obstacles to her growth — had been partially uncovered by her own creative search. They had begun to lose their power over her. The "big dog" in her dream that kept jumping on her turned out not to be so gigantic after all. Her own aggressive feelings, as represented by her own dog, Spot, had taken their place in that manageable combination of good and bad with which all of us human beings must learn to live.

As a last creation before she left the playroom with its special shelter, Jennie made a boat from cardboard and paper, no doubt as an expression of her launching out on her own into new waters. She pondered aloud what her boat might need. First she provided it with paddles, suggesting a means of directing it where she wanted it to go. She then added sails, so that her boat could get power from the wind; a cover of waxed paper for the hull, as a means of protection; and ropes, by which she could control the sails and manage her own journey.

After pondering her creation for a few moments, she said, "It needs something else." Her eye fell on a life preserver, a cardboard circle she had made earlier to supply a lovely pool-house that had been one of her renditions of finer dwellings. When she had made the life preserver, she had remarked, "The people in the house like to keep the life-saver where they can see it. You see, it saved someone a long time ago." In equipping her boat for launching, she suddenly decided that this life preserver should go along. Perhaps this paper circle alluded to the therapeutic relationship, which had provided assistance in the blooming of her own "bright affair," to return again to Dickinson's poem.

Jennie's long epic was made up of her own poetic renditions. It might be a disservice to the integrity of this very original work of art to superimpose on it all of the metaphors in Dickinson's poem. It is perhaps transparent, however, that in her own way Jennie used this garden plot of a play space, with an assistant with whom she felt safe, to pack further her own potentialities, to oppose successfully the gnawing conflicts that troubled her, to drink more deeply of the nourishment provided by an interested, uninvasive parental presence. By bringing angry feelings to the surface and by expressing these feelings through her own images, she was able to go a long way toward "adjusting the heat" that was making her so uncomfortable and so inclined to take cover behind a mask.

Viewing Jennie's therapeutic journey as a whole, we can recall her early comment about her caterpillars: "It would have been nice if they could have become butterflies." In fact, that is what had begun to happen to Jennie herself. "The bright affair" of her own play-work had been "so intricately done" in the nonintrusive presence of a mere assistant that she was enabled to offer herself more freely "as a butterfly to the Meridian," the larger world around her.

3. Henry

A Creative Young Mind in Doubt

Let me tell you about the Henry who appeared in my playroom some years ago.

Henry was a handsome, somewhat slightly built young nine-year-old, the first child in a family that stood in a long line of spectacular achievement. Grandfathers held high public office; his father was a highly successful businessman; his mother was a professional woman who had succeeded in a sphere that had been largely a male preserve. Excellence abounded and had always abounded.

At nine, Henry was beginning to have grave doubts about himself. He constantly devalued his ability and called himself "dumb" and "stupid." His confidence was lagging, and his school performance was beginning to reflect the results of anxiety and preoccupation with his feelings of inadequacy. His parents, alert to his distress, signed him up for a course of play therapy, agreeing to participate themselves in regular parent sessions so that we could all work together as a team.

The reports from school and the results of psychological testing revealed a bright child who was not performing as well as might be expected and seemed to daydream a great deal. We are already acquainted with this familiar educational lament. It goes something like this: "This child is not performing up to potential; has trouble focusing; is easily distracted; daydreams when he needs to be concentrating on his work."

This cluster of indices that a child has his mind on something other than what he is asked to focus on often falls under the diagnostic category of "Attention Deficit Disorder" or "Attention Deficit Hyperactive Disorder." It is perhaps my own bias that causes me to bristle somewhat at labeling children as "ADDs" and "ADHDs," perhaps because similar symptoms a couple of decades ago fell under the diagnosis of "Minimal Brain Dysfunction," and hundreds of children were categorized as "MBDs," an even more stigmatic label.

I do not presume to speak about all cases, but in my experience children brought to me for treatment with these diagnoses reveal over time that, far from being "inattentive," they are constantly attending to issues more pressing from their own point of view. Some of these issues are being unveiled by our three major cast members in this book.

Henry, like Jennie and Anthony, wrote his own epic drama over the months he came to play therapy. We might say that he has allowed us to attend his theater, where this epic was presented. What follows are are some of the episodes in the drama.

Prelude

In the first session, Henry was understandably puzzled. Why had his parents brought him here? Who was this new teacher sort of person who was sitting across a card table from him, not saying very much, only, perhaps, that it might be hard at first for him to know what he wanted to do here. "Sometimes children like to tell me about things going on in their families or at school," I said, "and sometimes they like to find things to play with and let me watch."

Interestingly enough, Henry took the unusual route — at first — of wanting to "tell me about it." That is the last thing most children want to do. But this child did, and he recounted that most of the problems for him had to do with his little brother. He wished his parents could understand him as well as they seemed to understand this younger sibling. He also mentioned his little sister, and told me a little bit about school, commenting that he didn't feel very smart at some things.

While Henry began talking about these things, he began to notice, and even to pick up, some of the various odds and ends lying on the card table: rocks, string, tape, sticks of various kinds, shells. As his sessions continued, he noticed some bits of fur — old tails that had come loose from an ancient fur stole that children had found uses for from time to time.

These bits of fur seemed to attract his attention. In the second session he had casually fingered one of these tassels and had attached one of them to a stick with tape, observing that it looked rather like a match, or maybe a candle. I followed and acknowledged this musing about a creation that had seemed just to happen, as though by accident.

In the course of my being with him, an interested observer, during this "happening," Henry mentioned that he sometimes used toothpicks when he made things and also that he had once made use of "science wire." I wrote down, in his presence, "toothpicks and science wire." For the following session I put a box of toothpicks, a role of insulated wire, and a wire stripper on the card table. Henry grabbed the wire and the wire stripper as though it were Christmas morning, and the session took off.

After experimenting with how to get the insulation off the wire and trying to master that delicate operation, he eyed those fur tassels again; I had added a number of different sizes to the pile, in response to his interest the week before. He mused to himself that if you had something to use for a head, you might make some kind of an animal from those tassels. I attended his inquiry as an assistant, and we fingered through a small supply of rocks, yarn, and shells in a basket of odds and ends, in search of something for a head. "I was leaning more toward an acorn," he said thoughtfully, "or something like that."

On further consideration, he thought that a shell might do if he could find the right one. He then hit on a candidate for the shell to use as a head — an elongated conical one — but he thought it needed some trimming at the end. That requirement gave us a mutual endeavor: to decide on a tool that might be useful to him. I wondered aloud if a nutcracker might serve, and his eyes lit up. For the next session I brought three kinds of nutcrackers, which launched us into Henry's successful enterprise of enhancing the end of the conical shell, into which he inserted the end of a fur tassel with glue, to his considerable satisfaction.

We might pause to ask, What on earth could be important enough about the apparently insignificant tinkering of a child with shells and fur tassels and the making of little animals to occupy the time of a professional and the investment of a family? Is it not ridiculous to suggest that the therapist and the child had stumbled onto something momentous in finding themselves jointly engrossed in finding the right tool for the trimming of a shell, so that the head of the animal came out to the satisfaction of the child? If this child was not doing his best in school, would it not have been better to be concentrating on his schoolwork? reviewing his math assignment? drilling him in vocabulary? What was so important about nutcrackers and shells and fur tassels and a collaboration in finding the right tool?

I will tell you what was important about this collaboration, and how it was that it served as the prelude to Henry's epic drama, which went a long way toward his solving the problem of his confidence and the effectual use of his gifts.

Following the Leader

The first point I want to emphasize here is how the child and the assisting adult were connected with each other. The boy, in looking for his own power, needed to discover his own thoughts and learn to hear his own signals, and to discover that an adult could follow him instead of lead him in that discovery. The willingness of the adult to follow him unquestioningly into what interested and concerned him, however minor it might appear to the casual observer, was the essence of the matter.

While parents and teachers are of course often obliged to lead a child, it is important in many circumstances to wait for the child's signals. The following, as opposed to leading, connotes acceptance of the child's spontaneous initiatives, of his creative impulses, of the train of his own thoughts. It suggests that something he begins without directive is worthy of respect, attention, and the time and involvement of the adult. It gives him confidence to follow a line of production on his own authority, and the respectful assistance of the adult reinforces for him the credibility of his own signals, encouraging him to follow further his original idea.

One might ask, How can we be so sure that the child's "own signals," his original ideas, are all that worthwhile? Could he not, after all, just be wasting time instead of going on to more important issues? In following him down just any byway, aren't we failing to teach him what are significant and worthwhile endeavors for his time and effort?

I believe that Henry himself will provide an answer to this question as we watch his unfolding drama. But let me say here that his search for the right tool with which to trim the shell was actually an important juncture in creating a safe space to sketch out the fears, hopes, conflicts, and desires that were preoccupying him. Here again, hidden deep within a child, was

43

an urge for growth and mastery that is resilient and powerful as soon as a safe space is found for it. The safe space was a relationship with someone who understood the importance of his fantasy and the need for concrete expression of that fantasy, someone who valued his images and was confident that where his own creative impulse was leading would be worth pursuing. The assistance of the adult in the pursuing intensified for him the weight of his own endeavor, and gave him courage to take yet another step along the chart that was forming itself in his own mind.

By the fourth session, Henry had completed his animal, which he did not name. He was happy with the way it looked, with the way that the glue had held the tail successfully within the conical shell, and he played with his animal, waving it about a bit. I told him that he seemed to be pleased with it, and he agreed. The way in which he waved it about gave me the impression that something within him was beginning to feel a little freer; something was beginning to stir, to move about.

External Clues to Internal Challenges

Pressures and Things Wobbly

The nutcrackers turned out to have further usefulness to Henry. As he experimented with the three nutcrackers that had been supplied, he began to muse about the qualities of each of them. One of them, he said, was quite "wobbly and unstable," and he proceeded to show me exactly what he meant.

"The wobbly and unstable" nutcracker is a perfect example of how readily a child will find a concrete object with which he can externalize what is going on within. In Henry's case, his comment provides clues about what lay behind the discrepancy between his cognitive abilities and his performance in school. Was he perhaps feeling wobbly and unstable himself? We do not as yet understand why that should be.

He began to examine the nutcracker that was composed of a metal bowl, with a screw designed to crack the nutshell. Henry wondered to himself — out loud — how much pressure something could take before it cracked. Thoughtfully, he rummaged around among the things on the table until an idea occurred to him. A cork caught his eye, and he put the cork in the nutcracker and turned the screw down on it with all his might.

The implication of this operation seemed to clarify itself when he said, "I want to see how long it can stand up under this." It became even clearer that he was speaking about his fears of how long he could stand up under the pressures bearing down on him when he squashed the cork and announced, "See, it just went flat," perhaps illustrating his own apprehension about being deflated in some way.

By putting the cork under the screw's pressure and smashing the screw himself, Henry could experience some relief from the position of feeling potentially smashed himself. He followed up this savoring of his position of power by undertaking to teach me a trick that he knew how to do with two sticks, a trick that, to his great delight, I had a genuinely hard time learning. When I continued to struggle with the hand maneuver and finally, after two or three sessions under his tutelage, succeeded in executing it, he jumped up and yelled triumphantly, "I did it! I did it! I finally taught you how to do it!" His joy in this success illustrates the satisfaction of being on the active rather than the passive end of things, and it gave Henry another thread of confidence in himself.

Sticks and Their Possibilities

We noted above how from the very beginning Henry saw the little wooden sticks on the card table as promising raw material for expressing previously formless ideas and feelings. He had begun with making that "match" or "candle" in the very first session. Could there have been some vague stirring that he needed more light shed on some things? Or was it about a form of power? Or about the need for something to ignite his own unused fuel?

Then one day, as though without consciously thinking of it, Henry began tying two rocks to a long stick. The endeavor was not a simple one, as the rocks were very uneven, and it was quite difficult to get them entirely surrounded by string and to get that string attached to the stick in such a way that it seemed to him "stable." However, Henry persevered in the way that children persevere when they are intensely interested in some undertaking.

While Henry was working with the stick and the two rocks, he was telling me about how difficult it is to make a sword. The following session he took two long sticks, and with great perseverance and ingenuity made a catapult, which, aided by a rubber band, could shoot paper across the room. One day I heard him running down the hall toward my office door for his session. As he sat down, he began immediately to think. Within moments he said, "I have an idea. With toothpicks, I could make a puppet — a miniature puppet." When he had finished creating a wee person from pieces of pipe cleaners and toothpicks, he mused aloud, "This could be Hector, or Odysseus maybe. It could be anybody I want it to be. I think it will be Hector." Then he proceeded to provide Hector with a bow, some arrows, a quiver, and a shield, which he covered with felt.

Henry explained to me, meanwhile, that Hector was the second-best warrior, but that he was "best loved by the gods." This clear reference to the situation with his brother and his parents was fascinating but opaque. Among other things, he said, "You know, gods are really not so different from people; they are people, really." Henry was delighted with his creation, and he asked if he could take it with him. "I can play with it on the way home," he told me. I wonder what fantasy of new power and bravery emerged as he played with his new puppet.

Sticks of various kinds presented themselves to Henry as ready material for expressing something that was important to him — something about power, about size, about prowess, about characters he had heard of who exemplified these things. One day he cut a wooden tongue depressor — a versatile material for him — into pieces and sat silent, pondering for a very long time. All I ventured was a comment that he was thinking. After a while, a breeze seemed to stir in his thoughts, and he asked for poster board. On this breeze entered a new theme.

Snails and Their Care

When Henry had the poster board in hand, he made some small round disks and, with some excitement, fashioned a little paper animal. He then pasted some tongue depressors onto a rectangle of paper, to make a kind of open box. He then looked up brightly — suddenly needing to go to the bathroom — but yelling to me before leaving the room, "I have a great idea for my snail!" When he returned, he was all "go" — his original mood had changed from lethargy to enthusiasm and energy.

Henry explained to me that at school, in a science project, each of them had a snail to care for. His sudden idea had to do with making up a menu for his snail. He eagerly engaged me in this project and wrote down the items on a piece of cardboard as he thought of them: snail salad, snail soup, snail hamburger. In the course of the task, he drew me a picture of the snail, which he rendered with striking competence.

Before he left that day, Henry explained all the cardboard creations he had made. One round disk was a "plate to feed his snail," and the toy animal was "a kind of dinosaur for the snail to play with." The open box was a carrier with which to transport his snail. At the end of the session I commented to Henry that sometimes it took him a while to know what direction he wanted to go in, but once he knew what that was, he could then go right ahead and carry out his plan. Henry agreed.

Snails. Snail food. Snail toys. A snail carrier. What on earth could all this mean? And how could it possibly be important to a child's growth?

In order to understand the significance of the snail's appearance in Henry's play, we need to digress for a moment to speak of some things we know about growing up. In order for children to pit their strength against the strong winds and excessive heat and invasive worms that Dickinson speaks of in her poem, they have to do a great deal of packing in nourishment — or, in the words of the poem, "obtaining their right of dew." Just as muscles require protein and other good things over the years to be able to function well, the heart and the mind require nourishment too.

All of us creatures know about this nourishment. Puppies know about it; kittens know about it; little lambs know about it; and all of us human children know about it. There is a great hunger in every creature for tenderness and warmth and softness, a hunger that was to some extent met and to some extent not met in the earliest hours at the breast or in the arms of a caring guardian.

When we are chronologically grown up, whether we need a moderate or an exorbitant amount of this nourishment largely depends on how generously the need for it was satisfied at that time in life when it was most urgent and necessary — that is, in infancy. But regardless of how much of it we were fortunate enough to receive, none of us ever completely outgrows a recurrent thirst for the goodness of the maternal breast in its larger sense and whatever paradise of plenitude that the era of the breast supplied.

In suddenly being inspired to give thought to the tender care and feeding of his snail, Henry was responding to that place deep inside himself that yearned for more of this elixir; a part of him sensed that these matters underlay his efforts to grow stronger. In assuming the role of caretaker and addressing the "baby needs" of his snail, Henry had rediscovered the same ingenious solution mentioned above. That is, he could be in the *active* position and dispense the caring as a way of vicariously receiving it himself.

Parenthetically, this solution — to try to give to others what one is yearning for oneself — is an often-used and sometimes overused way of attempting to satisfy the hunger for the elusive sweets of early childhood.

For now, let me underscore that what Henry was doing for his snail was extremely important for his work. It was in undertaking the task of growing up that he turned briefly to the theme of satisfying the needs for tender care and finding a way to symbolize them. It was not an accident that during this period of snail-feeding he thought wistfully of children with AIDS, "whose parents just go off and leave them in a hospital."

Henry was certainly not neglected by his parents. His mother breast-fed him faithfully during his infancy when she was at the height of professional training pressure. His father, even though he was a hard-driving businessman himself, had always been conscientious about the needs of the family, sometimes at considerable sacrifice to his own personal interests. When these perceptive parents observed that their child was suffering a lack of confidence in himself, they took on the task of setting up some therapeutic help for him that involved substantial commitment of time, money, and dedication to investigating the tides and currents of the groundwater underlying the life of the family.

Henry's feeding of his snail was followed by an entire series of creations having to do with the growing-up needs of his adopted animal. He always began his sessions by thinking. One day, as he sat quietly at the start of the session, his eyes looking thoughtfully around the room, he suddenly had an idea. He reached for a piece of poster board and began drawing two large circles on it with a pencil — one circle inside another. After he had completed the circles to his satisfaction, he announced to me, "Maybe my snail needs some exercises to get in shape." The circles were an exercise track for his snail! At first Henry seemed satisfied with the efficacy of the track for his snail's workout needs, but after more thought, he began adding something to it. He took some wooden tongue depressors and began gluing them around both sides of the track, in order to make walls. Apparently his snail needed firmer boundaries; Henry explained that he added them "to help it stay on the track better."

For some weeks, Henry devotedly created helps for the welfare of his snail. He made a house, a house for traveling, and a "house for staying still," as he described it. He also made "a tunnel for underground" in this "house for staying still," as though snails, like boys, might need a place for subterranean thoughts and feelings that couldn't always manage the public air. Dickinson wrote a poem that captures this feeling:

Best Things dwell out of Sight
The Pearl — the Just — our Thought.
Most shun the Public Air
Legitimate, and Rare

Dickinson, #998

It is often surprising to adults that children, when they speak of such things as a snail needing guides to stay on track and a house for staying still, are so guilelessly speaking of themselves without being aware of it. Henry did not consciously know that he was speaking of developing his own "life muscles" and being able to keep himself more effectively on track. Most significantly, the creations he brought into being around the theme of growing up were themselves helping to bring that growth about. As Richard Sewall put it, "The poet doesn't just make the poem; the poem makes the poet." How this comes to pass is a primary theme of this book.

It is striking how frequently children use the idea of a snail to express the sense of the emerging self, with the spiral cavities somehow representing the spaces yet to be filled. Both Henry and Jennie carefully drew the snail's spiraling cavities; Jennie remarked once, wistfully, "I love to draw those things."

Generating Power

One winter day, Henry realized — with glee — that he could generate electrical power on the rug in my office. He discovered the electrical charge he could get by making friction with his feet on the rug and then touching the radiator and seeing and hearing the spark. He also "plugged it into" me by generating the charge and then touching my arm to see if he could see a spark. His enthusiasm for this game was unbounded. He would try touching the radiator after a once-around-the-room scuffing and watch eagerly to see if he — and I — could see a spark. He continued to up the ante, first scuffing once, then twice, then three times, then expanding the endeavor into the other room and scuffing some more. When he came to the great moment of touching the radiator, there was suspense and excitement. Would we see a spark? Would we hear the connection? Could I see the spark? Was I sure that I saw it?

To experiment with augmenting his power and observing the impact of it, especially with my participation and admiration, was a game that Henry must have found especially rewarding, because he returned to it again and again throughout the course of his work.

Going Faster and Further and Hitting the Mark

In the many months that followed the work described above, virtually all the themes which found expression had to do with this idea of developing and expanding Henry's sense of forcefulness. There was a plethora of images that he began giving concrete form. Most often he expressed this theme of power by creating stronger and more versatile weapons. He created impressive bows and arrows and swords and crossbows and catapults, which he constantly redesigned and improved.

One example of this metaphor was a very interesting weapon with three blades. Henry got the idea to create it at the end of a series of sessions he had used to make a Viking ship. He came in one afternoon and was very clear about his agenda. He asked for the piece of cardboard he had been drawing on the week before and proceeded to make a three-part blade with one convex outer part and two convex inner parts that came to a point, reinforced with a wooden stick. Then he made two others like the first one and asked for a metal brad, a fastener, that would enable him to put all the parts together in such a way that they would be movable. This flexible design enabled him to fold up the weapon and put it into his pocket.

I inquired about how he saw the advantages of this weapon. He showed me that it would go farther when he hurled it across the room, that it would go faster than his previous designs, and also that the blades "would have a better chance of meeting their mark with all those curves." This invention was just one of a long series of stronger and better weapons, once conceived as a huge sword built from balsa wood featuring a hilt attached with real nails. At the height of the sword-making era, Henry brought to his session a huge metal replica of a real sword some four feet in length, complete with a long scabbard, which his parents had given him. The task he set for himself in this session was to clean and polish this emblem of strength that he was building and that I was to help polish and admire. My only role here was to be an attentive assistant and silently understand the message he wanted me to hear: that he was proud of his growing prowess.

Of War in the Fortress

It may seem as though Henry is presenting us with a straightforward, unopposed assuming of a potent, more forceful role for himself. But the road to making oneself felt is not so simple. As Henry began to experiment with ideas about making himself strongly felt, he also began to feel counterforces. One day he mentioned aliens and spoke about his aversion to them as he began idly to sketch some ugly little creatures. "They are terrible," he said — "not the drawing of them, but the things themselves. I can't stand to look at them. What if you opened the door, and there they were?"

We have to ask, Who are these aliens by whom Henry feels threatened? Ordinarily, when children are dealing with monsters, we think first of those feelings within the child himself that he is finding too large to handle, usually anger at the ones he loves. The condensation in the image of the monster no doubt also includes the parents themselves, or, rather, the internal representations of the parents that merge with the child's own aggressive, angry feelings. What makes them alien? Is the alien part the sense that one cannot easily master and integrate these troublesome impulses, and therefore one wants to distance oneself from them, to put them not just out but way out, and make them as foreign as they can get — namely, alien?

We are all put together in very much the same way, and it would seem that children from a very early age struggle with the conflicts between wanting their wishes fulfilled, the anger that inevitably accompanies the frustration of the wishes, and the guilt feelings that the anger engenders. Since these conflicts are difficult for even the most grown-up of us, we can understand that it is even more difficult for young children to cope with these troublesome matters.

We have come to speak of these ways of coping as defenses, and, interestingly enough, children in their play often use literal fences as a way of picturing for themselves this need for protection against the conflicted currents of feeling. In Chapter 8 in Part III, I will take up these issues in more detail. Here I bring up the matter of "defense" to help us understand what Henry did next.

One day, in the midst of glorying in his creations of increasingly powerful weapons, Henry began thoughtfully to do something else. Having just completed a chariot for the Hector figure he had made, with which he seemed quite pleased, he asked if there might be a shoe box around. The shoe box began to take on the features of a medieval fortress. First Henry went to work on making a gate to the fortress, and he spent a great deal of time arranging for the opening and closing mechanism of this gate, as though the means of controlling the entrances and exits were of paramount importance. Then he began to glue tongue depressor sticks all around the fortress, asking me to help hold the freshly glued sticks in place until they were strong enough to stand by themselves. His enlisting me as his helper in firming up his defensive structure brought to my mind that phrase from Dickinson's poem: "assisting in the bright affair." The bright affair here was his wresting from deep inside himself the means to bring to the surface and work with the warring factions in his feelings.

One day he built a platform high up inside the fortress, on which all the little knights that he had constructed of pipe cleaners and toothpicks could stand securely while sighting and firing at their enemies. This platform near the top seemed to position his armaments at the perimeter of his defensive position, a kind of eyes and ears near the surface. He would sometimes ask out loud, "Now what do I do next?" He would look at me sometimes as though he thought I might have an answer. When I would respond with, "I guess it hasn't come to you yet," that seemed to give him courage to take the next step. This time, he exclaimed, "I know — a weapons rack!"

Henry's first attempt at making a weapons rack of slitted cardboard with toothpicks sorely disappointed him when the toothpicks all fell out, but this setback quickly gave way to renewed enthusiasm when he discovered a way to make a catapult from a metal soda-bottle top glued to a tongue depressor stick. Completed by a paper cup as a foundation and a rubber band ingeniously secured to an extension on the top, the catapult had real movement and real power. Henry was highly pleased with his creation when he discovered that he had inadvertently made two weapons in one — a catapult and a battering ram. The idea of the battering ram grew into a much larger project during the following session, when Henry carefully constructed out of cardboard a rectangular, elongated tower in which he inserted a heavily fortified battering ram that had a great deal more heft than the first one.

The fortress and its accoutrements were Henry's rendition of his attempts to defend himself in the midst of internal conflicts and to come up with some certainty about that ability to defend himself. Certainty, however, is one of those wishes that for all of us is doomed to be frustrated. The battering ram may well have been an introduction into the scene of self-doubt and the pressure of guilt feelings that were battering him in the face of his aggressive — and, as we will see — sexual strivings. A sense of "There is something wrong here" seemed to pervade the play, a subtle introducing of punitive messages permeating the pleasurable certainty of power. As a late thought, Henry added a moat and a drawbridge around the fortress, an ingenious extension of control over what was and was not to be allowed into his container of feeling.

Fish, Fishtraps, and "a Bird That Just Fits into Its Cage"

As Henry approached the age of twelve, other themes started to emerge. He created a cleverly designed trap to catch fish, or, he said, "it could be to hold a frog." He took great care with the details of this slatted structure, giving special emphasis to the hinges to facilitate the opening and closing of the trap and a string that would determine how far the trap would be allowed to go down into the water. Henry said that one of the advantages of his fish trap was that the fish wouldn't get hurt.

I was puzzled over this matter of the fish trap. Was it about not being the fish and therefore not getting caught in other people's traps? Was it about Henry's own ability to capture and hold something secure? Was it another image of the containment of impulses?

An intriguing detail was his expressed concern about minnows getting in and eating up the bait and keeping away the big fish. It occurred to me that such an allusion to little fish and big fish in contest over the bait might not be far away from a reference to the triangular contest which, as we have seen, so plagued our young friend Anthony. What Henry turned to immediately after the fish trap may give us some further clues.

After he put aside his fish trap, following much experimenting with it in a basin of water, he sat one day in a long period of silent thought. He said he was unsure about what he wanted to do, but then stated suddenly, "I have an idea. Cage-smage." Brushing aside my interest in the word "cage-smage," declaring that it was not important, he made a small container out of tongue depressor sticks. "It's not really a cage," he told me. "You can't know what it is because it isn't anything real at all." He then made a clay animal and showed me how "it just fit" into the container. This cage for a little unidentified animal was followed by a series of containers made of clay, culminating in a bird's nest into which "just fit" a clay bird.

It began belatedly to dawn on me that these creations might be unconscious renditions of a budding sexuality that Henry felt safe to handle in this setting where he could know that his boundaries were not going to be stormed. This realization was confirmed by what came next. Henry produced a series of artistic creations that depicted mountains and rivers and gorges in three-dimensional landscapes that were part painting, part sculpture. The mountains were built up on the picture with clay. These artistic renditions seemed to have an almost kinesthetic quality, as though touching and feeling them, as well as seeing them, were tangibly suggested. A delicately wrought flower carefully penetrated by a long stem further elaborated the sexual theme. We will return to this subject when we consider the task of "adjusting the heat," which all children must confront in the handling of aggressive and sexual urges.

Viking Ships and Submarines

It is striking how often children employ the image of a boat or a ship to express for themselves their own Odyssean prospects. As we have seen, Jennie summed up her entire work of play therapy in the creation of her boathouse, followed by an outfitted frigate to launch herself out to sea.

Henry also used two different versions of this metaphor. Shortly after completing his fortress, along with its powerful battering ram, he decided to produce a ship — a "Viking ship," he announced. Some of the details of his concerns about his ship reveal how clearly he was speaking about enhancing his own seaworthiness. "I hope to make the bottom waterproof," he said, and he spent more than one session experimenting with different materials that would keep his boat from leaking in its testing ground of the lavatory. He showed similar ingenuity and patience in designing and executing the prow of his ship. He did not expand on the importance of this aspect, but it suggested to me the point of his impact on his world.

Henry commented that the mast would have to hold everything up, especially the sails, which "would catch the wind and give the ship power." He also emphasized the importance of the anchor as he designed and made it from an old arrowhead, explaining to me that before they had invented the anchor, "they would have to get out of the ship, take ropes, and pull the craft up onto the beach." He expressed concern about not making the rope that held the boat too short, "because if a strong wind came while the boat was anchored, the wind would blow the ship over." This intriguing line will reappear in Chapter 6 in the context of "eluding the wind," that phrase from our guiding poem which refers to the particular task that requires children to learn to stand up against the breezes and the gales that inevitably assail them.

Henry stressed the importance of battle strength for his ship, explaining to me in great detail how "the Vikings or someone invented a narrow bridge that could rest inside their own ship, but could be thrown out to reach an enemy ship with a sharp spike." He created this sharp spike very skillfully with a toothpick, showing me how it could simultaneously hold the other ship and crash into its exterior, enabling his warriors to overcome the enemy ship. This reference to aggressive power (which, I have noticed, has such an important role in many of the games that children, especially boys, play) reminds us that aggression is an essential component of all of us, and that learning to claim it, curb it, and utilize and direct it is one of the most challenging tasks of growing up. All of the weapons Henry made during the course of his work were references to this necessity of dealing with his own aggressive strivings, without which not even a daffodil could push its way through the earth.

About three months after Henry's experimenting with the various potentialities of Viking ships, he had a further marine inspiration. One day he announced, "I know what I can do, but it will take a long time." After thinking for a while, he asked whether I might have a piece of transparent but firm plastic that could be seen through and would bend. We located a plastic container that seemed to be promising, and he told me that it would be something like Roman glass that you could almost see through.

As he began to put wooden sticks and duct tape together, Henry explained to me that he was making a submarine, and he began to sketch on paper his thoughts about its design. It was to be an "old-fashioned kind of submarine," powered by human energy rather than engines. He drew me a picture of where someone would sit in the submarine and pedal, as on a bike. This arrangement would give the craft power and at the same time would allow for steering with a kind of propeller to give the craft direction. He invented an ingenious turnable propeller with some metal brads holding its components together. Apparently, provision for maneuvering was an important feature of the vessel.

"There would be someone up on on the bridge," he told me, as he sketched this idea into his plan, "to tell the boat where to go and all that." In this statement I heard him referring to the executive part of his own self that he was trying so hard to make stronger. He then began to elaborate on all the things he would need to design and build in. He would need to make the vessel tight, he said, and began to add clay to patch the holes in the balsa wood so that water would not leak in. He decided to have a section "made of skins and other fireproof material in order to be able to build a fire for cooking and stuff." There would also need to be a way to keep things cold. "Can you do that by wrapping things up?" he asked. Do we have here, once more, an allusion to that matter of "adjusting the heat"?

"Then," Henry said, "there would have to be a tube, so that the person could breathe, and a periscope, so that he could see what was up above." Also, there would be rocks — heavy rocks — to put in the ship if the commander wanted it to go down, but a way to unload them if he wanted the ship to go up. Particularly important was the transparent plastic Henry had requested, which would provide a kind of underground window. When I asked about the advantage of this, he said, while demonstrating his point with gestures, "If you had a piece of wood right here in front of your eyes, it wouldn't be too good, you know." Apparently, seeing all things clearly would be important.

An anchor was the next important enterprise. Then there had to be a weapon, which Henry designed as a log that could be shot up out of the submarine to defend it against any ship that threatened it. He also mentioned painting the bottom of the submarine red so that it could be distinguished from the other ships.

Henry Brings Us into Port

Henry spent many weeks working out, executing, and testing the various aspects of this ingenious creation that externalized his internal concerns.

He wrote his own poem, so to speak, about strengthening parts of himself to stoke his potentialities, supporting his images with concrete, tangible objects, as children always do. He gave thought and expression to the need for human energy and power through the submarine's pedals, to the need through the steering, and to the need for guidance and direction through the commands "from the bridge," that internal authoritative voice he was gradually taking over from the original parental source.

His tightening of the submarine's surface so that water wouldn't leak in surely speaks of the intactness of the boundaries between himself and the world, and his provision of oxygen and food represents his way of speaking about obtaining his "right of dew." And what imaginative renditions he made of the need to regulate the heat and the cold, to defend himself against external threats, and to increase his ability to see things clearly!

Henry's poem about equipping himself for the scary business of growing up uses different materials from those in Dickinson's poem about the flower's responsibilities, but the latent meaning is strikingly analogous. It is interesting to note how his imagery about launching his own boat parallels Jennie's at the close of her own play therapy.

One interesting feature of Henry's poem was the summing up his enterprise in terms of a submarine rather than a ship. He seemed to be giving voice to some sense that the work he was doing was taking place deep inside himself. The frequent dream of people in therapy that they are in subway trains or basements strikes the same theme of a subterranean life that goes on without our being aware of it.

One of the hundreds of ways that Dickinson spoke of these "underneath" parts of ourselves explains why we go to such lengths to keep them veiled, why we go near them only when they are veiled, as in dreams, and why children put them into poetry:

. . .
Far safer, of a Midnight Meeting
External Ghost
Than its interior Confronting —
That Cooler Host . . .

Dickinson, #670

* * *

In Part I, Anthony, Jennie, and Henry have each shown us how they were taking responsibility through the seriousness of their play for their own deepest concerns, for struggling with the influences of their "old-fashioned ghosts," for confronting and working with their own aggressive and sexual strivings, for building strength to cope with threats from without. In short, they have revealed to us glimpses of their part in the "bright affair" of growing up.

In Part II, I will continue to employ Dickinson's poem about "bloom" as a lens for further examining what these children have brought to us in the hope of better understanding what facilitates growing up.

II. Seeing the Children's Presentations through Dickinson's Lens

Here again is the poem that provided the literary germ from which this project grew, and which now serves as something of an outline for the second section:

Bloom — is Result — to meet a Flower
And casually glance
Would scarcely cause one to suspect
The minor Circumstance

Assisting in the Bright Affair
So intricately done
Then offered as a Butterfly
To the Meridian —

To pack the Bud — oppose the Worm —
Obtain its right of Dew —
Adjust the Heat — elude the Wind —
Escape the prowling Bee

Great Nature not to disappoint
Awaiting Her that Day —
To be a Flower, is profound
Responsibility —

Dickinson, #1058

4. The Family as the Main Garden

Before considering the poem's specific metaphors, let us take note of the implicit garden in which all these matters of flowering can occur. We need a view of the garden itself, and also of its crucial nutrients.

Family: Some Observations

Revealing in play therapy their yearning to be seen and known and understood, children intuitively and unconsciously start to convey some message about the family. I think of one little girl who, when informed of the impending divorce of her parents, picked up markers and spontaneously drew a sphere divided into two colors. Clearly unaware of the allusion, she spoke of separating a world into two parts. Another child, upon seeing her family breaking apart, drew a picture of herself as a bug, apparently seeing herself as the lowly creature at the bottom of it all.

Yet another child, whose family was intact but troubled, made a family out of the play dough, commenting that "it is a floppy family, a weird family, a wacky family." We recall that Anthony, unwittingly depicting his family as made up of the sun, the moon, and two other planets, accentuated the line between cold little Pluto and the sun, remarking that "Pluto gets his power from the sun," perhaps suggesting some feeling about the importance of his connection to his father. Another little boy, in his very first session, represented the four members of his family as four pipelines made of clay, about which he said, "There isn't anything flowing in there."

The centrality of the family is prominent in most schools of thought concerned with human development, and the same is true in much of great literature. Harold Bloom, for example, points out,

> The deepest conflicts in Shakespeare are tragedies, histories, romances, even comedies, of blood. When we consider the human, we think first of parents and children, brothers and sisters, husbands and wives. . . . We think of families as being alone with one another, whatever the social contexts, and that is to think in Shakespearian terms.[1]

We know that the family in our society is under siege by social forces both at the top and at the bottom of the economic scale. The institution of marriage is clearly straining at its seams, not only because of social forces, but also because of those unconscious ancient ghosts bringing the miseries of past generations into every new family. While society has not always offered the present alternatives to marriage, the power of those old ghosts haunting every family has ever been thus. This observation, attributed to Carl Jung, pertains: it is only when we see whole families literally destroyed that we come to understand the power of the unconscious complex.

However, there is another side to the matter. The family, as rocky as it is, and as subject as it is to erosion, to flood, and to the disintegrating forces of our society, is still the main garden in which the young have a chance to grow up to be sturdy plants in their own right. Marilynne Robinson tells us about the extraordinary resilience of the family:

> Families will not be broken.
> Curse and expel them, send their children wandering,
>   drown them in floods and fires,
> and old women will make songs out of all these sorrows
>   and sit on the porches
> and sing them on mild evenings.[2]

We are touched by — although unlikely in our present milieu to recreate — the picture of families William Blake made in "The Echoing

---

1. Harold Bloom, *Shakespeare: The Invention of the Human* (New York: Riverhead, 1988), p. 733.

2. Marilynne Robinson, *Housekeeping* (New York: Farrar, Straus & Giroux, 1981), p. 194.

Green." Here we see the old folks laughing away care while they watch the young play on the same green where they in youth had also played, and the sun descending on the peaceful scene:

> Till the little ones weary
> No more can be merry. . . .
> Round the laps of their mothers
> Many sisters and brothers,
> Like birds in their nest,
> Are ready for rest. . . .[3]

What Does "Family" Mean Today?

In our present century the family is in a state of redefinition, and it is not so obvious what constitutes the kind of loving, nurturing garden in which children flourish. There may be literal, biological families that function poorly or not at all as nourishing soil for the young, and there may be a growing number of stable, nontraditional groupings that provide more effectively for the emotional needs of children than some of their more traditional counterparts.

For the purposes of this book, we will define the essence of family as a set of daily, dependable, home relationships in which a child can come to feel loved in such a way that this force translates itself from the passive position of being loved into the active position of loving.

What follows is an approach to what characterizes such relationships.

The Central Hypothesis of This Book: Beyond Deserving

Parental love and, by extension, all mentoring love is authentic and effectual in proportion to the degree that it transcends the commonly assumed principle of the circular exchange. All true love is a stranger to "this for that." The "justice" idea of reward according to what is deserved is replaced

---

3. William Blake, "The Echoing Green," in *The Poetry and Prose of William Blake*, ed. D. V. Erdman (New York: Doubleday, 1988).

by the much more powerful force of uncontingent, compassionate alliance *with* the essential personhood of the Other, however small that part may appear to be, and *against* the destructive forces opposing that person's good.

Hamlet provides us with a good example of such destructive forces and the need to understand that those beset by them are themselves among their victims:

> "Hamlet is of the faction that is wrong'd;
> His madness is poor Hamlet's enemy."
>
> *Hamlet,* Act V, Scene ii, Lines 249-50

The Offense of This Radical Departure from a Basic Tenet of Social Living

As human beings, we are much more at home with relationships that function — overtly or covertly — on the basis of quid pro quo, the essence of which is simple: "You do this, and I will reciprocate with something good. You don't do that, and I will repay in kind." As much as we dislike thinking of ourselves as living by this crass kind of exchange, this model actually permeates most of our relationships. As intimate partners, we may think we are freely giving our time, devotion, and service to the other, without a calculation of recompense. However, haven't we all, at the least expected moment, found ourselves in a situation where we feel withheld from, disregarded, or underappreciated? (And if you live close to another person, you don't get through a week without someone feeling this way.) At this point, don't we sense something rising in the gorge — whether or not it is held firmly behind the teeth — saying, "After all I've done!" At the very least, we are likely to require a repayment in the form of stated acknowledgment and gratitude for our generosity, as a reassurance that we are "good."

This is one homely example of how the model of the circular exchange permeates our experience of human interaction. The mutual seeing, the mutual hearing, the mutual service, and the mutual gladness that we would like to think characterize our personal relationships do not easily escape this regression to the endless variation of good for good, and some version of righting something that has been wronged in the world by replying in kind.

Any annulment of this arrangement seems to assault something deep within all of us, some principle that must be originally based on the law of the talion: an eye for an eye and a tooth for a tooth. However much we dislike it, we find ourselves responding in this way, according to this standard. We feel that people should reap what they sow, get paid in kind for what they earn. In fact, our social, educational, justice, and penal systems are, by and large, based on this model. There is an entire school of psychology, still popular on many fronts, that builds its philosophy on manipulating a child's behavior to please the adult by holding out rewards for compliance and withholding those rewards for noncompliance. However benign and "non-punitive" the system appears, the child, of course, experiences in the latter case a form of punishment.

It is clear that, in suggesting that there is a kind of loving that resists setting up a circular exchange as the nature of human relationship, we are running up against a world set up on that very exchange. However, the three children discussed in Part One have demonstrated that the common assumption that "deserving reward" or "not deserving reward" is effective in rearing children is trumped definitively by a love that cannot be earned at all.

My personal sense of this important difference, which may not be shared by everyone, is that the kind of love we deliver to our children, the love that feeds the heart and mind, does in fact model itself after a dimly perceived sense of the way divine love comes to us — that is, as moving in upon us *first*, without any presupposition of our deserving or earning anything. Shakespeare speaks of this difference in a scene between Hamlet and Polonius. When Hamlet instructs Polonius to see the traveling actors "well bestowed," and Polonius replies, "My Lord, I will use them according to their desert," Hamlet responds, "God's bodkin, man, much better! Use every man after his desert, and who shall 'scape whipping? Use them after your own honor and dignity; the less they deserve, the more merit is in your bounty" (2.2.531-32). This pronouncement rings true to us (although the idea of "merit" in the last phrase still has in it that troubling problematic of quantification of deserving). Nevertheless, with our children we find it difficult to put Hamlet's advice into practice without feeling that we are somehow abdicating our parental duty.

We actually all started out giving this kind of love to our children. Take Wordsworth's immortal picture of the young child in "Ode: Intimations of Immortality from Recollections of Early Childhood." When he wrote, "With light upon him from his father's eyes,"[4] he was not speaking of a conditional approval.

Not one mother among us ever offered her breast or its surrogate to her newborn infant with a condition laid on the gift, nor have I ever heard of a father withholding his attention from a newborn until he or she "deserved it." It is true, however, that infants can give parents a sting, can wound their self-regard, so to speak, if they don't nurse plentifully or give the parents some reassurance that they are being good parents.

Let us pause here to explore whether a parent needs to get something back from the child even to grant the gift of this earliest nourishment. It is not uncommon in psychotherapeutic practice to hear from hurt, empty adults who say that they got the message early on that they were bad babies, that they did not satisfy their parents' needs and wishes, and that they were in general felt to be deliberately troublesome, even around feeding issues. I remember hearing an exhausted mother of numerous offspring, whom she had tried to rear along with their own numerous offspring, sigh, "I've brought all these children into the world, and not one of them has done anything for me to show me any gratitude."

Usually, however, it is later on when the "this for that" model seems to infiltrate the garden with our children. It is when aggression starts to rear its ugly head, or what we parents experience as stubbornness, uncooperativeness, laziness, or other non-pleasing, non-compliant behavior, that we are tempted to employ the reciprocal exchange model. I don't know of any parents, personally, professionally, or socially, who haven't at some time or another sunk to bribing a child to get something accomplished — however euphemistically it was presented. A new toy in exchange for a good grade, a subtle salary of some kind for putting the poop in the potty, or — always under the guise of parental wisdom — an enforced loss of a pleasure in response to displeasing the adult.

If we were to entertain the notion that the most potent form of parental love does not depend on children's behavior, compliance, or what has been earned or deserved, how would it affect our efforts to bring them up as responsible, caring, accomplished individuals? In practical terms, how would a model that is not based on the "this for that" model work in

4. William Wordsworth, "Ode: Intimations of Immortality from Recollections of Early Childhood," in *The Selected Poetry and Prose of Wordsworth*, ed. G. Hartman (New York: Meridian, 1980).

daily encounters with our children? How would we teach them to brush their teeth or share their toys or improve their manners? How would we help them to achieve whatever they are supposed to achieve — all the way from mastering pull-up pants instead of using diapers to getting ready for the SAT?

Let it be very clear that I am not advocating a simplistic stance of permissiveness with children. The subject here is a parental presence that is certainly not passive, that is in fact powerfully active, and that is firmly inclined to intervene on behalf of the child when intervention is needed. Departing from the deserving model does not mean abandoning children to their impulses. When a child is at the mercy of impulses and wishes that are not good for him, the most powerful intervention lies in a firm and decisive *stopping* of the hurtful behavior. The issue is where the intervention comes from. Does it derive from *the most powerful force in the world — love that is conditionless?* Or does it derive from the weaker force of a need to enforce one's own will on this other being through manipulation, whether of promised rewards for compliance or threatened punishment for defiance?

"That is not good for you; I have to stop you" entails different appropriate actions at different ages. At four, it may mean removing a stick from a little boy's fist, or removing a child from a situation altogether, "until you have better control of your hands." At eight, with little girls in an unstoppable catfight on an outing, it could mean "That's it, girls. We don't have it together enough for a trip today. We're going home, and we'll try it again another time." At fourteen, a comparable stance might be, in response to a young girl's really indecent attire for a party, "No, you may not go in that outfit; it's not good for you. It's not going to happen."

I admit that enforcing such a stance in the latter case may well be a tricky matter, and the pros and cons of issuing an ultimatum to an adolescent need to be carefully weighed. (What parent has not issued an ultimatum only to regret it when a battle royal emerged?) It is good to avoid a power struggle whenever possible, and often it is better to put the child on the "executive committee" and ask her questions about how she would feel if her choice were overruled.

The major point here is the *radical difference* between this kind of discipline and the "If" kind of discipline. "If you don't stop that, you get no television tonight." "If you girls don't behave more kindly to each other, there will be no ice cream." "If you leave here in that dress, you'll be grounded for two weeks."

The position of an unconditional stance on the parent's part does not mean, of course, that there are never any consequences for out-of-line behavior. The temporary loss of a toy that a child can't manage until he can handle it better; the end of an outing without the ice cream; the missing of the party when the fourteen-year-old is adamant about her skimpy outfit — these are painful consequences, and the child is likely to feel them as "punishment." However, they are not based on a punitive, retributive idea of justice or on a parent's manipulation of a child; they are based on a strong parental love that will not succumb unwisely to hurtful behavior.

A sagacious love that moves in forcefully to stop something is as different from punishment as is freely offered generosity from the manipulation of a child's will. "If you get your homework done, you can have a treat" is manipulation. "You seem to be having a hard time getting started on that paper. Would it help to have a milkshake first?" is reaching out in supportive, non-earnable love.

It is manipulative to say, "If you do what we want you to do about college, we'll buy you a car"; it is an expression of power, not of love. But it is an expression of non-manipulative love, the most powerful force in the world, to say, "We've made it clear why we feel that so-and-so would be the better choice here. But if you disagree, we're confident that you'll consider carefully all the pros and cons before making up your mind. We'll support you, whatever you choose to do, to whatever limit we can afford."

In the next chapter, on the nature of the "assisting role," I will explore further specific examples of the implementation of this more powerful kind of intervention and how it differs from permissiveness.

The task at hand is to further explore some of the qualities of the kind of love that is trying to make itself known in these pages, and to address the mystery of its sources.

The Qualities of Non-Manipulative Love

What are the key qualities of non-manipulative love? Here, drawing on the work of Karl Barth, I will explore these qualities in some detail.[5]

---

5. For the qualities of the kind of love under discussion in this section, I am especially indebted to Professor Christopher Morse of Union Theological Seminary, who made these insights available to me through the writings of Karl Barth. These qualities of love as I dis-

Givenness

As implied in all that has been said above, this love is like the dew that just "comes," unsummoned. It moves first, and it cannot be earned.

To the extent that we are able to give this kind of love, we have already been given it ourselves. We inherit whatever propensity we have for it from someone else: mother, father, grandparent, or some other benevolent source. It is exceedingly difficult, if not impossible, to give what we have not received. This fact discourages the stingy soul, but it also reminds those who are able to be generous and giving that they can take little credit for these capacities. This is not to say that people cannot develop such capacities; otherwise, writing a book like this would be pointless. Nevertheless, it remains true that manufacturing or contriving a giving spirit simply out of a wish to have one is a doomed endeavor.

Participation

This love *enters into* the Other's distress, as opposed to standing over against it, which is the deeper meaning of the word "mercy."

If we move for the moment from speaking about parents and children to speaking about grown-up intimate partners, we may be able to understand better the difference between a stance *with* and a stance that is *over against*. With couples, it is sometimes hard for one person to enter into the other's hurt and suffering because the wife may think, "He's brought this on himself," or the husband may think, "What did she think would happen if she took that kind of risk?"

To be able, as a partner, to enter into the other's pain without judgment or blame, and to attempt to *understand* it in the light of the other's own past and through the other's own eyes — that is *mercy.*

Of course, this quality of love can also take a material form. A drink of literal water, a needed gift of money, or a timely, thoughtful reaching out to another with concrete assistance is not being dismissed here as irrelevant. But the accurate grasping of what the other is feeling, and the finding of words to deliver the understanding as empathy, is often how love is most powerfully felt.

---

cuss them here are a secular rendition drawn from Barth's "Perfections of the Divine Loving," Chapter VI, Rubric 30, *Church Dogmatics* II/1 (1957), pp. 351-439.

"With all that's weighing on you, I know this fight we're having is the last thing you needed today." To be able to say this to a partner or to a friend is an example of this quality of being able to enter empathically into the sphere of another — although few if any of us could offer such kindness, especially if we were angry ourselves. Nevertheless, I have known specific instances of just such a powerful balm to break through an absolute impasse in a marital squall.

To take this matter of "participating with" back to parents and children, how might such a gift be given to a child who is behaving in such a way as to drive the parents to distraction? Let me give one illustration of parents who were able to "enter into" their child's suffering as opposed to judging and punishing her behavior.

This story is about a little five-year-old girl whom we will call Susie, who had always had trouble sleeping through the night. She predictably awoke and came to her parents' bed about one in the morning and cried inconsolably until she was allowed to stay with them or until one of them would come and lie down with her. After trying all the methods of stopping the child's behavior currently approved by authorities, the parents agreed to a course of play therapy with me, with the mother and child both coming to the sessions. Both parents were eagerly involved in wanting to help their little girl, but, as often happens, it had become clear through exploration that the primary locus of the troubling conflict and ambivalence was with the same-sex parent.

The mental suffering that this child was going through, the torment that was waking her up at night, soon became evident. In the first two sessions Susie took delight in the play dough that Jennie (in Chapter 2) and countless other children had discovered as a resource, and she basked in the interested and exclusive attention of the double mother presence in the room. Through making and serving play-like cookies, pasta, pizza, and so forth for her mother and me, she satisfied poetically her yearnings for more of the tender maternal care and nurturing — that "good breast" — the hunger that none of us ever completely outgrows. As the therapist, I mainly served as an amplifying presence to intensify the nonjudgmental, exclusive attention of the mother and to heighten the child's absorption of this condensed version of her mother's profound love for her.

Most young children begin a course of play therapy by revisiting in some form this earliest stage of development in what we may call the paradise of the mother's warm breast.

Before we examine what this child did next, it needs to be clear from the outset that the cruel nature of the drama that unfolded is not to be taken as revelatory of how she herself was being treated by her devoted parents. It had to do with something inside herself, not so uncommon in young children, that I will explain below.

Turning one day from the play dough to the Barbie dolls, Susie enacted a series of parties for the girls. Each week all three of us were given a doll to dress up for the party, and all the necessary supplies were provided for the festivities — a record player for music and dancing, for example, and a table for refreshments.

However, a "marplot" — that is, a spoiler of the plot — immediately entered the scene. One of the dolls — first the doll that Susie's mother had, quickly replaced by mine — had to undergo again and again the pain of being left out of the party and relegated to her bed. Not only was the luckless outcast made to be sick, but she was told, "I hope you get worse."

This was only the prelude to the fate awaiting the unfortunate doll. In the second rendition of this drama, the doll was informed that she had to be harpooned or killed and finally had to suffer both of these cruel fates. The other dolls were required to get weapons — knives, swords, and other deadly arms — and attack the victim until she was dead. As a final ignominy, little toy bugs were placed on her lifeless body.

As the theme of cruel and unusual punishment got further developed by this talented young scriptwriter, we began to see that she was enacting scenes in which she was struggling with all her might to deal with a mysterious and intolerable conflict.

Could it be that this conflict was similar to the one that wrestled in the soul of young Anthony (in Chapter 1), who showed us so vividly what it was like to suffer from wishes for something that could not rightly belong to him, and to endure terrible guilt feelings about those wishes? You may recall that his bank robber had to battle the forces of justice over and over before he could be relieved of his need for punishment for his crime.

Susie answered this question over a period of weeks. In her artwork and in game after game of her own design, she portrayed the torment in her soul. What emerged were scarcely disguised murderous feelings toward her mother, that same mother who loved her dearly, whom she loved passionately, and on whom she was dependent for her very life.

Shocking? Perhaps, or at least it seems so until one has been in a position to witness regularly over many years this same kind of play in quite normal girls and boys — play in which an oppressive authority figure is assassinated by a subordinate. Not surprisingly, the murder is always followed by an appropriate punishment for the criminal, as we saw in the repetitive dramas cast by Anthony. The imagery that children use in these dramas could often be compared with all the bloodiest and most barbaric features of the fairy tale, which also needs to be understood as in keeping with the primitive sense of justice in all young children. From time to time I have witnessed in such scenes everything from dismembered victims to cannibalism, expressions of normally developing youngsters who are trying to come to terms with their own ambivalent feelings toward a loved parent. These played-out fantasies involve what they dimly sense as intense wishes for some illicit satisfaction, terrifying guilt regarding the horrific means that would be necessary to experience fulfillment of these wishes, and a murderous rage toward the parent who is sensed as frustrating the wish.

Susie's rendition seemed ingeniously to combine in one act both the elimination of her perceived rival and the logical death penalty for herself, which she enacted through execution by electric chair. Her very cooperative mother was chosen as the victim to be tied up in the rigged death chamber and repeatedly subjected to lethal shocks until verifiably dead. The child resourcefully found just the right prop for her imagined instrument of justice: an unused doorbell button that gave her perfect control over the moment of lethal electrocution.

Some might say that this is just a remote, incredible, outmoded Freudian notion that no one believes any longer. In these days of the science of the brain and sophisticated medicines to help children sit still and "focus," surely such ridiculous ideas can have little to do with what children are suffering in their minds.

My primary point in this section is that these parents were able to *enter into* their daughter's suffering by bringing the child into a therapeutic situation, which helped them both to bring new family forces to bear on the worrisome situation with Susie.

The mother, who was on the front lines, so to speak, worked energetically to understand what was occurring in her daughter's unconscious mind that was producing the symptoms of irritability and sleeplessness. She was willing to enact repeatedly the part of the bad mother — the witch, for the purposes of the child's drama — not an easy task for any mother. But she thus enabled Susie to bring to the surface her excruciating feelings, giving them external form in this accepting situation, and in her play to use all the ingenuity of the creative unconscious mind in order gradually to find relief from her torment.

One example of this intriguing imitation of the dream is the way Susie could easily shift the parts of the drama around, causing the unwanted "badness" to be represented by different parties. All of us are able to do such rearrangements in our dreams, thus owning and disowning simultaneously impulses that are unacceptable to us. This perception helps us to understand that the severe punishments Susie inflicted on the "bad" party (usually her mother or me) and the constant scoldings and reprimands (e.g., "You wretched little rat!") that she doled out in her play were both serving an important hidden purpose. These were renditions of what she felt she herself *deserved* from her mother, rather than a reflection of what she actually received.

The latent idea here is this: "Given that I want what belongs to my mother, and that I am trying to steal it from her, this must be what she feels toward me and what I deserve." How immortal is that eye-for-an-eye and tooth-for-a-tooth principle in children's minds, to say nothing of most "adult" minds (not exempting governments and heads of state).

Over time, Susie and her parents were able to alleviate her distress by that particular aspect of love we are calling "participating with," in lieu of punitive action to enforce the parental will.

Of course, not every parent is called upon to deliver mercy in this particular way in a therapist's office. Being able to participate in a child's inner woes is an art that is most often developed when parents themselves are young and have a model to teach them about these matters during their own childhood.

This principle of understanding a child's woes by entering into them — or, differently put, by imparting *mercy* — shades readily into the third quality of the kind of love we are groping for: an attitude of *patience*.

Patience

When applied to our dealings with our children, this word has a stronger meaning than our ordinary use of it, which suggests the ability to bear up under the aggravation of other people's perversities. Patience in this context means that the parent knows how to wait, how to accompany and sustain the child, allowing space and time for the child's own being to emerge without coercion. Its presence is kind (as Barth suggests); it does not inundate or swamp. Like mercy, it takes a position *with* the other rather than a position that is *over against*.

This patience allows this other creature to develop with regard to its interior integrity — that is, in *freedom*, freedom to become its real self, according to its own latent interior design. This freedom is to be distinguished from a permissive stance which suggests that "anything goes." A notion of freedom that implies such license is not freedom at all. To acquiesce in the unlimited gratification of a child's every wish or urge, with no restraint, is to abandon him or her to a different kind of tyranny. Nothing is more frightening to children than to feel that there is no larger container for their impulses than their own as yet underdeveloped inner controls.

For a long time, the parent *is* the holder for those feelings and urges that are too overwhelming for an infant or a child to handle alone. Gradually the child internalizes the management and control first supplied by the parents, and when those have become firmly incorporated into the self, the external authority of parental figures is no longer required. Indeed, it can become deleterious for a young person's development and needs to be relinquished. I will say more on this subject in Chapter 5, where I distinguish parental *assistance* from parental *control*.

Here are two illustrations of the difference between accompanying and sustaining a child with *patience* and enforcing the parental will by manipulation or coercion.

Recently I heard a heartrending cry pierce the air in front of the grocery store. A terrified little girl who was about three years old was refusing vehemently and with all her might to get back into the stroller that would return her to the nursery school. It apparently seemed to her to be a matter of life and death to stay out of that cart that was to take her, like French nobility, to her private version of the guillotine.

I have wondered ever since what transpired in this contest of wills between the daughter and the mother, who was ineffectually screaming, "All day long you have wanted to go to school, and now you are acting like this!" The mother was as out of control as the child, and her feelings were as poignant. She was furious too. The volume of her voice was only slightly lower than her daughter's as she insisted that the child give in and go to school.

Here is another picture, a more extreme one: A mother once came to my consulting room to discuss the "eating problem" of her sixteen-month-old child. Bluntly put, the child was refusing to eat. The mother told me how the parents were being taught — by their church, no less — "to bring up an obedient child." I have not yet had the courage to look into the guidebook she mentioned, but the general ring of it was to bring up the child by coercion to submit to the supposedly superior will of the parent. "Breaking the will of the child" was the stated, chilling goal of these false teachers, who were advocating spanking the child until she gave in to her parents' wishes about when and what and how much she should eat.

I do not blame these misguided mothers. They were as caught in a web of tyranny as the children, and it was not their fault that they had been given an erroneous map.

What would a stance of "patience" in these two instances mean, in practical terms, and what difference might it have made if these two mothers had been given such a gift themselves?

Patience in these instances would not mean communicating to the first child that she would never again be asked to go to school, nor to the second child that if she wanted nothing but ice cream and cookies, that would be all right. It would mean attempting to *enter into* the picture in such a way that these other beings felt heard, understood, sustained, accompanied, and helped.

Had patience been in the first mother's repertoire, for her little girl it might have taken the form first of comforting her, holding her, and encouraging her to say what was scary about the school. Then the mother would need to acknowledge her daughter's terror. "I understand that it's just too scary for you to go to school right now," she would say, "and we won't try it again today. I'm going to help you with this, and together we'll find some ways to make it less scary."

The next task would be for the mother to ask the school's teachers what they had observed about her little girl's fear and to design with their help some more gradual supportive approach to her learning to separate from her mother by increments of mastery. In this situation, compulsion only aggravates the problem and leaves the child feeling abandoned by her sole source of support.

The second mother was also herself in need of assistance. In her intention to bring up a "well-behaved" child, she was failing to recognize this other being's interior integrity and give her the room to emerge and de-velop according to her own internal signals. Patiently "sustaining and ac-companying" this interior development would mean neither allowing the child to have unlimited junk food nor serving as monitor and dictator to the child's appetite. That this sixteen-month-old had an "eating problem" — and indeed, she was "on strike" — was a transparent indication that the parents misunderstood their appropriate role.

An important question arises at this point. If family relationships, in order to transcend the deserving model, need to have these qualities of un-conditional and prior movement toward the child, the participation with (rather than the judgment of) the pain and suffering of the other, and the patience to sustain and accompany this other creature without coercion, from where does this kind of love arise?

Sources of Non-Manipulative Love: Differing Conceptions

While there would seem to be an inevitable divide between those who feel that such love must derive from a divine source beyond the human sphere and those who believe that the human spirit is itself sufficient to supply it if families and other circumstances are favorable, this difference is often bridged by poetry or some other art.

The poet laureate of these pages, Miss Dickinson, had many ways of silencing such arguments by seeming to include or transcend both posi-tions. Who of any philosophical position would not be disarmed, for ex-ample, by the following:

> I reckon — when I count at all —
> First — Poets — Then the Sun —
> Then Summer — Then the Heaven of God —
> And then — the List is done —
>
> But, looking back — The First so seems
> To Comprehend the Whole —
> The Others look a needless Show
> So I write — Poets — All —
> . . . .

Dickinson, excerpt from #569

Elsewhere, Dickinson dispels these differences in a similar way while speaking directly to our present subject — that is, what nourishes growing creatures — by using one of her frequent references to the metaphor of water:

> I know where Wells Grow — Droughtless Wells
> Deep dug — for Summer days. . . .

She goes on to mention the poem that she reads in "an Old fashioned book" about people who "thirst no more" and waters that "sound so grand," and she concludes,

> I think a little Well — like Mine —
> Dearer to understand —

Dickinson, excerpt from #460

Dickinson had a very modern sense that the doctrines and the myths that sustained our forebears seem to many to be emptied of their power. In one love poem (#587), one senses that her reference to "Eternity's vast pocket, picked" points beyond the loved person to other "Heavens stripped."

Nevertheless, we see from the Dickinson canon — in such words as "Eternity," "Immortality," and "Infinity," which she seems to use almost interchangeably — that she was also deeply imbued with a sense of what lies beyond human capacity. Here is but one example:

> Of Paradise' existence
> All we know
> Is the uncertain certainty —
> But its vicinity infer
> By its Bisecting
> Messenger —

(#1411)

What she meant by lines like the following is, as always, left to the reader to discern:

> The Well upon the Brook
> Were foolish to depend —

Let Brooks — renew of Brooks —
But Wells — of failless Ground!

(#1091)

William Blake, whom I quoted above in connection with families, was frequently iconoclastic and skeptical of authority. Still, he never hesitated to speak theologically. In "The Divine Image," we read,

Where pity, love, and Mercy dwell,
There God is dwelling too.[6]

The Bible, so frequently associated with rules and laws and retribution for wrongdoing, is actually a rich and varied source of expressions of the extraordinary kind of love not built on earning, or what I have claimed is devoid of a circular exchange based on deserving.

There was a Hebrew songwriter who was very clear about such *hesed*, this steadfast loving-kindness, naming those very qualities of prior givenness, mercy, and patience described above, declaring,

The Lord our God is merciful,
and He is gracious,
Long-suffering, and slow to wrath,
In mercy plenteous.

He will not chide continually,
nor keep his anger still.
With us he dealt not as we sinn'd
nor did requite our ill.

The Scottish Psalter, #103, emphasis mine

Such a song elicits in us a longing to be able somehow to experience such a love and somehow to echo it in our dealings with "our neighbor," although it would seem to stretch us beyond our natural inclinations.

The prophet Hosea, after first depicting a wrathful, punitive God raging against an unfaithful, adulterous Israel, then speaks of God as turning away from his anger at their wrongdoing, saying,

---

6. William Blake, "The Divine Image," in *The Poetry and Prose of William Blake*, p. 13.

I will heal their waywardness
and love them freely,
for my anger has turned from them.
I will be like the dew to Israel;
he will blossom like a lily. . . .
He will flourish like the grain.
He will blossom like a vine. . . .

Hosea 14:4-5, 7, NIV

Our modern sense of justice is still based squarely on the this-for-that model. Accordingly, when we turn from these Hebrew poets to the New Testament, we find analogous passages contradictory to our way of thinking. I will explore a few of those passages in Chapter 7. Here it is sufficient to mention one: Romans 11, where Paul announces that God's mercy is more powerful than the human capacity to be disobedient (Rom. 11:30-32).

These are examples from a book very often conceived as a restrictive moral code of some kind. On the contrary, it is in essence a radical declaration of the end of "merit" altogether. As uncongenial as this may be to our sense of justice, anyone who has ever been touched by a relationship that is not dependent for its mercy on deserving knows its power to alleviate rage and anger.

Freud, contemptuous as he was of any religious belief, was himself ultimately to say that human existence comes down to a war in the Heavens between Eros and Thanatos. He later amended the thought by adding this question: "But who can foresee, and with what result?"[7] He was skeptical, apparently, that love was going to prove more powerful than the forces of aggressive destructiveness, but he seemed to have arrived at a position that required a reference to something beyond the human mind.

I personally embrace the radical faith in the ultimate victory of love — that is, the kind of love described above — over rage and hate. I will return to this matter in Chapter 7, "The Snake in the Garden."

---

7. Sigmund Freud, *Civilization and Its Discontents*, standard edition, 21 (London: Hogarth Press, 1961).

5. The "Minor" Role
of the Garden Assistant

Returning to Dickinson's poem about the nature of "bloom" quoted in its entirety in the introduction to this section, we consider its intriguing metaphors as they are germane to the process of the flowering of human beings.

In this way we see the poet's surprising assertion that the gardener — the analogous parent, or teacher, or therapist, or mentor — is a "minor Circumstance" who does no more than *assist* in the "Bright Affair." The profound responsibility for becoming a flower lies with *the flower itself.*

Here we are reminded that the gardener does not make the flower happen. A human creature is not ours to form as we like; this being has a great deal of independent life of its own.

What are the implications of this poetic warning? First of all, it tells us that one tries to find out what is already going on in this other creature. There are important matters already happening when we meet up with a new little being, and we need to know about them in order to cooperate with the forces for growth already budding, so as not to get in their way. "Plant a radish. Get a radish. Never any doubt," says the song in *The Fantasticks.* It tells us that the unfolding of a plant will happen according to its own internal design.

To be sure, the same song reminds us that there are unforeseen complexities in the human sphere. When the songwriter concludes that "with child-er-en, it's bewild-er-in'," and that "once you've planted child-er-en, you're absolutely stuck!" he accurately expresses what some parents feel most of the time and what most parents feel some of the time. Assisting in the child's growth is a daunting undertaking; but we begin by noting that, in addition to coming into the world with an inborn potentiality, children are, in the main, hardy, resilient creatures. They naturally strive to be full plants. If they hit a rock, they will try to grow around it. They will also reach for the sun, as does every flower. If they miss a drink of water, they will urgently keep reaching for it. Indeed, the urge to keep reaching for a missed drink, that "right of Dew," is part of the child's profound responsibility that is our subject, and that fact is altogether reassuring: we have a minor rather than a major role in this assisting task. How, then, does it happen that the business of rearing children is frequently so fraught with difficulty?

Fi, fie, fo, fum! Is That Giant in the Attic after Me? Am I a Bad Parent?

One of the primary obstacles to our assuming confidently this minor-but-important role as assistants lies not with the child but with us as parents. If a child does not eat vegetables or go to bed willingly, or if the teacher says that Billy is shoving the other children around and can't "focus" on arithmetic, we understandably feel that the difficulty must somehow be our fault.

Many of the parents who have come to me about some problem with their children suffer from this lurking fear that the difficulties stem from some flaw in themselves. Few of us feel that we have fully arrived at being beautiful and mature persons, and our own sense of imperfection complicates the task of assisting our children. As usual, Dickinson knew what to say: "Lest I should insufficient prove/ . . . [is] The Chiefest Apprehension/ Upon my thronging Mind" (#751).

To be sure, an internal critic is a necessary companion in living. The question is whether our internal critic is mild-mannered and gentle, like Jiminy Cricket, or is severe, ruthless, and tyrannical, like Jack's famous giant in the attic, who keeps showing up in this book. In the latter case — far more common in the human family, especially among parents — the thundering voice in the mind can roar at us and threaten to devour us, emotionally speaking. For every human being, altering the volume of the roar is one of the major tasks in growing up.

In Chapter 7 I will consider the matter of fault and blame in some detail. Here it suffices to point out that "It isn't your fault" is as important a message to parents as it is to children. Softening the internal accusatory voice in family members, in ourselves, and in our friends is one of the clearest communications of the particular kind of love that lies at the heart of this book.

The Big Snag: "The past is never dead. It's not even past."

This well-known quote from Faulkner's *Requiem for a Nun*[1] illuminates the big snag in our own growth, and especially in our parenting: none of us starts with a virgin plot of soil.

This statement would be mainly a positive one if all of us had had most of our own vital needs optimally supplied when we were growing up — that is, the needs to be cherished, treasured, seen, heard, and understood by parents who had been given the means by their own parents to deliver all this, along with the requisite provision for material and bodily sustenance.

The rub lies herein: even the most fortunate of us, who had many of these vital needs well-supplied when we were young, are still struggling to obtain more of them for ourselves when life has brought us to the task of supplying them to the next generation. And for those who, because of deprivations in the past, are trying to nurse the young from empty emotional wells, the vocation of nurturing can prove to be discouraging indeed.

That the old is present in the new was stated aptly a long time ago: "The fathers have eaten sour grapes, and the children's teeth are set on edge" (Ezek. 18:2). The same venerable source has told us about a snake that showed up in a garden and caused a lot of trouble. We will hear more of that story in Chapter 7.

Apparently, there is no way for us to start over. We live in an infinite series of mirrors that keep reflecting what was there before. In *Moby Dick*, Herman Melville was making a similar statement when he said, referring to Ahab's suffering in the violent displacement of his ivory limb, " . . . all the anguish of that then-present suffering was but the direct issue of a former woe; . . . that . . . the most poisonous reptile of the marsh perpetuates

1. From REQUIEM FOR A NUN by William Faulkner, Ruth Ford, adapter, copyright 1950, 1951 by William Faulkner. Copyright 1959 by William Faulkner and Ruth Ford. Used by permission of Random House, Inc.

his kind as inevitably as the sweetest songster of the grove."[2] We will revisit both Melville and Faulkner in another connection in Chapter 6.

Children seem to have some primordial sense of what these writers are saying. To wit: one little boy I worked with saw "a skeleton that is about a hundred years old" buried in the clay trap he had built. Another child showed me about ancient material by using old, discolored blocks to build the bottom layer of his prison for his bad guys, and using new, bright-colored ones to build the top layers. He remarked that the foundation had been built first and had been there for a longer time, and that the old blocks would show that better.

Anthony, whom we met in Chapter 1, unaware that he was speaking of old familial forces, once drew a picture of icebergs that "had been there such a long time that it was impossible to thaw them now." Jennie's "old-fashioned ghosts" may well have referred to antique presences whose power over her she sensed, and in her play she used these puppet ghosts to symbolize her struggles for freedom from them. At the end of her drama in the playroom, she destroyed one of the ghost puppets and "buried" the other one in a bottom drawer of a playroom chest, as though she were conscious that those old forces were to some degree immortal.

This theme of inevitable recapitulation in the present of much that would seem to be buried in the past will come up again in Chapter 7 in connection with the matter of that snake in the garden. In the present context, my emphasis is on how this reality complicates the assistant's role in bringing up a new generation of human creatures to "bloom."

Returning now to the series of evocative metaphors as they appear in the guiding poem, we begin with bloom.

Bloom: What Would It Mean in Human Beings?

The first word of the poem, "Bloom," already arrests us with a question. When a flower blooms, the "result" is visible and self-evident. What would it mean for a human being to bloom? Of the many ways one could think about it, what comes to my mind — especially in the light of working closely for many years with persons of all ages struggling to arrive at such a state — is Freud's famous five-word answer to a similar question: "to love

2. Herman Melville, *Moby Dick* (New York: Penguin, 1992), pp. 505-6.

and to work." This unexpectedly simple reply to a question about what a normal person needs to be able to do, according to general agreement, has never been improved on.

Love: Some Definitions

As soon as such a word as "love" is mentioned, we are of course faced with the formidable task of indicating what it means. Love can scarcely be defined in any one way. We can only walk around it, as we might walk around a mountain, and point to various features clearly or dimly perceived.

If we asked what the poet catalyst for this book had to say about it, we might be walking around this mountain for a very long time. But in one of her most succinct and pithy definitions, she says,

> Love — is anterior to Life —
> Posterior — to Death —
> Initial of Creation, and
> the Exponent of Earth —
>
> Dickinson, #917

As usual, Dickinson doesn't make it easy for us, but she seems to say here that love begins before life, continues after death, is that which begins creation, and that which multiplies the meaning of ("exponent of") earth. That is my reading; there must be many others, especially of that enigmatic last line.

The uses of the word "love" are so myriad as to render it almost powerless to communicate a particular meaning. The word can refer simply to finding qualities in something or someone very appealing, engaging, or attractive, resulting in a strong regard for or predilection toward that person or thing. We can say that we love a certain kind of music or art or poetry, or even ice cream, meaning that these things please us repeatedly and satisfy us in some way.

Then there is the love that is felt as erotic passion toward another person in either a transient or a more long-lasting emotional state. We can involuntarily "fall in love" with someone, and the euphoric pleasure experienced in being with this other can become almost inexplicably all-encompassing and necessary to our existence. This is the eros of sexual love that dominates romantic literature, has an important place in nearly all literature, and saturates the visual media, from advertising through genuine drama.

In life partners of advancing age we can observe something that binds them together in a constancy and faithfulness to each other that can only be called love, although euphoria, sexual passion, and even joy may be long gone. We hear repeatedly at weddings Shakespeare's much-honored words: ". . . Love is not love which alters when it alteration finds . . . but bears it out even to the edge of doom" (Sonnet #18). While few of us perhaps can claim to know any such thing, it rings true to us.

Frequently we use the word to describe a feeling of warm affection and attachment deriving from natural ties, or sympathy, or the experience of caring for another being, such as a pet. Love can refer to being concerned about, feeling drawn to, and impelled to extend oneself toward friends, or to more idealistic concern about one's neighbor, in the wider sense of others not in our immediate personal circle. The outpouring of compassionate feeling toward massive human suffering — to victims of earthquakes, floods, and the ravages of war, for example — would exemplify the meaning of the word.

This capacity to be concerned about those who may not be useful to our own interests, who evoke our kindness and generosity in an apparently "disinterested" way, begins to stretch our understanding of the reach of this word. The idea here is that love in this sense is not contingent upon the other's deserving or inclination to reciprocate, and at its ultimate limit includes even one's enemies. The mystery of such uncontingent love is the primary content of Chapter 4. It is also the thrust of the major hypothesis of the book (spelled out there), and it will continue as its major theme.

This kind of extraordinary love precisely not predicated on a circular exchange found one of its most moving expressions in the poetry of the prophet Hosea:

> When Israel was a child, I loved him,
>   and out of Egypt I called my son.
> The more I called them,
>   the more they went from me. . . .
>
> Yet it was I who taught Ephraim to walk,
>   I took them up in my arms;

but they did not know that I healed them.
I led them with cords of human kindness, with bands of love.
I was to them like those who lift infants to their cheeks.
I bent down to them and fed them.

Hosea 11:1-4, RSV (1925)

"Those who lift infants to their cheeks" and bend down to them and feed them are among those for whom this book is written — both those who do so literally, with their own children, and those who care for and nurture other beings in various ways, such as those who care for the sick and weak and unfortunate. Further dimensions of this mighty word "love" will emerge as we proceed. For now, it is simply our point of departure in describing a major feature of "bloom" in a human being.

Work: That Other Aspect of Bloom

Since the Oxford English Dictionary requires nearly four columns of microscopic print to "define" the word "work," it might be useful to cull out for ourselves an idea of how it is to be used here. For a start: *Work* is the exertion of effort toward some end, such as planning, making, producing, composing, or building something for a purpose. Put somewhat differently, to work is to bring about an effect through the performance of some task or process or course of action.

Children's Play as Work

If we think back to the course of play therapy presented to us by Anthony, Jennie, and Henry, we can see the natural impulse of children to move spontaneously to the undertakings mentioned in the above definition. Anthony began his therapeutic "work" by planning how to make a faulty airplane go "higher," and followed that up by making a picture of a cannon with difficulties analogous to those of the plane.

As soon as Jennie felt safe in taking charge of her time in the playroom, she began sketching and developing plans for the construction of a house, which grew into sustained efforts toward further aims known only to herself, and perhaps at that point not yet fully known even to herself.

Her creations not only expressed and gave form to the concerns that gradually emerged, but also enabled her to take action to address them.

Henry wasted no time in reaching for odds and ends on the playroom table to begin to make things, and the course of action that he undertook over more than two years of "work" in the playroom moved through successive stages of artistic creations that he employed toward ends of his own, of which he himself was hardly aware, and which were revealed to me only gradually.

In his "Ode: Intimations of Immortality from Recollections of Early Childhood," Wordsworth offers us a timeless perception of the child's play as work:

> Behold the Child among his new-born blisses,
> A six years' Darling of a pygmy size!
> See, where 'mid *work* of his own hand he lies,
> Fretted by sallies of his mother's kisses,
> With light upon him from his father's eyes!
> See, at his feet, some little plan or chart,
> Some fragment from his dream of human life,
> Shaped by himself with newly-learned art,
>   A wedding or a festival,
>   A mourning or a funeral;
>   And this hath now his heart,
>   And unto this he frames his song:
>   Then will he fit his tongue
> To dialogues of business, love, or strife;
>   But it will not be long
>   Ere this be thrown aside,
>   And with new joy and pride
> The little Actor cons another part. . . .[3]

3. William Wordsworth, "Ode: Intimations of Immortality from Recollections of Early Childhood," in *The Selected Poetry and Prose of Wordsworth*, ed. G. Hartman (New York: Meridian, 1980).

Enemies of Work

If, as it seems to appear from watching children at play, work seems to be such a natural, spontaneous impulse in the first part of life, we might wonder what sometimes gets in the way later on that can render work into an unpleasant burden? Why do some grow to dread and avoid work as though it were an enemy instead of something to be reached for? And why do some find themselves unable to work, or severely inhibited from doing the very thing that clearly establishes for others a source of satisfaction and a firm place in one part of reality, the human community?

There is no doubt that social forces favor only a part of our society with opportunities to develop natural gifts and personal interests within a nurturing educational environment, which makes work more intrinsically appealing. That millions of others must struggle for the barest means of survival and have little or no access to those opportunities would explain a part of the widespread aversion to work, especially if work is limited to the menial, the noxious, and the underpaid.

However, people who grow up with an aversion to work are by no means limited to the oppressed classes, and some in the oppressed classes find satisfaction in whatever work is available to them. This fact suggests that there must be other factors involved.

The children have given us an eyeful of what interferes with work. Anthony, Jennie, and Henry, as well as most of the others I have known in the playroom over many years, were brought to see a therapist because something was askew at school. "My child is said to daydream too much" or "can't seem to focus well" or "doesn't pay attention in class" or "can't seem to concentrate" or "isn't achieving up to potential" or "dawdles over his work" or "won't do his homework." These and other similar reports seem to alert parents and teachers that something elusive is impeding academic work.

When these signs begin to be reflected in poor achievement reports and bad grades, the reactions vary. Some parents and teachers start to push harder, some resort to the time-honored (but dubious) stick-and-carrot approach, some scold, some deny that any problem exists — and some seek enlightenment about what is going on and find out what it means to "assist" as opposed to direct or to drive.

Investigating what might interfere with a child's work toward this desirable end often discloses unexpected roots. Sometimes even very good parents are surprised to learn that their child has a vague notion that work is not a self-owned enterprise; rather, it has come to be primarily a benefit for Mom and Dad and Teacher. If these "assistants" of the child have an excessive personal stake in the excellence of the work, a development that is difficult indeed for parents to avoid, it can certainly produce a hidden conflict in a child's mind. Whose business is this, anyway? Is homework, for example, designed to enlarge the child's bank account or that of his elders?

Adults can prevent such a distortion early on by making sure that children get the message that they are on the executive board of any business that involves them, whether it is how many ounces of formula are needed for a meal, how long a practice session at the piano should be, what clothing choices can be made, what subjects call one to maximum effort, and many, many other issues that arise in the course of growing up.

The guiding poem for this book offers us splendid metaphors for what children themselves have to do, and the next chapter will focus on the various facets of their own responsibility for such matters as packing their own buds for future blooming and opposing the worms — that is, the conflicts within that keep gnawing at them.

In this section, I will mention only briefly, in connection with understanding the assisting role, how some of these conflicts may interfere with work. The adult who describes the child as "unable to focus," "inattentive," or "wasting time on irrelevant matters" may not realize that the child may simply be focusing on and attending to what for him are more important and pressing issues than what the teacher is presenting.

Often what preoccupies a child is a deep concern about whether he is going to be "enough," or, differently stated, whether the task at hand will add to his stature in his own and others' eyes, or whether it poses a danger of diminishing that stature. It is not unusual for a child to avoid work so as not to expose himself to the possibility of losing that wished-for stature.

In addition to these formidable foes, it must be added that any enemy of immediate pleasure, such as reality impinging on our wishes for some gratification, has to be contended with in understanding these matters. For most people, the satisfaction derived from fulfilling work is less intense than the direct gratification of an impulse or a wish. There is a reason why Pinocchio's struggle to resist the appeal of Pleasure Island so that he could become a real boy is a timeless story.

These various factors by no means exhaust the subject of impediments to fulfilling this important part of life, but they do offer us a beginning in better understanding them.

The Relationship between Love and Work

For children, learning (and, by extension, work throughout life) has as much to do with feelings — and very particularly the feeling of being loved — as with cognitive abilities and cognitive stimulation. Regardless of how much helpful light science brings to the latter, we ignore the former to the peril of our young. The primary poet of these pages, in her usual enigmatic way, put it this way:

> The Mind lives on the Heart
> Like any Parasite —
> If that is full of Meat
> The Mind is fat.
>
> But if the Heart omit
> Emaciate the Wit —
> The Aliment of it
> So absolute.

Dickinson, #1355

All children yearn for the presence of a parent, initially the mother, who can be with them in the way they need that parent to be there. In the previous chapter, where we focused on the qualities of a powerful love, we spoke about givenness — that is, love that moves first and is not based on earning; participation, or entering into the other's distress as opposed to standing over against it; and patience, or sustaining and accompanying the other without coercion.

Children would not be able to put into words these ways in which they need those gifts, but they have a powerful radar that senses when these features of love are present as well as when they are absent, and the wish to experience them in their parents is immortal. When this wish is fulfilled, a child is freed to do his work — that is, to learn; when this wish is thwarted, a child is angry about the frustration of this most basic need, an anger that may interfere not only with school tasks but with all of the business of life. A child may completely block out any awareness of this rage, but it can burn on and on within the mind and wreak its havoc, not only on the capacity and motivation for work but also on the capacity to give and receive love.

For a number of years I worked as a psychologist in a psychiatric hospital. There I was able to observe some of the most striking examples of how children require a relationship in which they feel loved before they can focus their minds on learning.

Indelible in my memory is a love-starved seven-year-old boy whom I will call William. He began his academic career with a sullen refusal to participate in any learning situation in his classroom. At the outset of a course of play therapy, he told me unequivocally, in response to a question of mine, that what he was good at was "hitting people in the face." He had found this particular expertise to be much more effective in making his way in the world than any other pursuit offered to him, and he was indeed quite formidable in applying it.

Elsewhere I have recounted in some detail how this child moved from this position to an eagerness for the nurturing to be had through books.[4] Stated more succinctly here, it was through the weekly infusion of the nurturing of a caring parental presence that he began to find a connection between that experience and the stories that were read to him. His teacher reported that his first flicker of interest in class was warming to a story she had read aloud, which he asked to hear over and over. It was about a little boy who couldn't grow up "until he had done something wonderful."

What I also noticed was a change from his original aversion to a circle of children sitting on a blanket with me, listening to stories. A bad little monkey whose faithful friend always forgave him for his misdeeds, the man in the yellow hat, and a horse whose troublesome, powerful sneezes were transformed into a heroic deed — there was something about these stories that called to him very persuasively. His resistance gave way to a hunger for more and more such stories, and his teacher reported that he began reaching for books and was learning to read.

---

4. Dorothy W. Martyn, *The Man in the Yellow Hat* (Atlanta: Scholars Press, 1992), pp. 25-33.

"Beyond Deserving" Assistance

When I speak personally with parents or teachers about active intervention with children in a line of assisting that neither relies on a this-for-that model nor takes a permissive stance toward any kind of behavior, I like to draw a picture. The picture consists of a simple stick figure that illustrates — in a somewhat oversimplified way, to be sure — how, as human beings, we are all put together. I draw a line down the middle of the stick figure and sketch on one side a cloud of tumult, similar to the image given to the cartoon character Pigpen by Charles Schulz.

This part of the picture is meant to allude to the *impulse* side that resides in all of us, the urges, strivings, sexual and aggressive feelings — in short, all the energetic pulls and pushes in us without which we would be in effect lifeless. There is in fact a more or less magnificent horse in us that gives us the power to go and to do and to live vigorously, but that also can get us into trouble when it takes off without our permission — that is, without the supervision of thought and judgment.

An example that comes to my mind has to do with a bright four-year-old who, in the temporary absence of the supervising adult during a family feast day, undertook with his chubby, competent hands to choke his little cousin — in response, no doubt, to some internally valid rendition of an eye for an eye and a tooth for a tooth. I will speak later to the appropriate parental response to this runaway impulse, which here only serves to illustrate the infinite possibilities of young horses without bridles. Of course, it doesn't have to be a young horse to qualify here. Who of us in the course of a week does not find our judgment lagging behind some impulse that proves after the fact to have been misguided?

On the other side of the divide in my stick-figure rendering, I sketch in a visual representation of the *manager-control* part of the person, which looks a little like a chambered nautilus. That is, I draw a tiny, embryonic layer that represents how small this management part is in early childhood, and I try to show how, during growing up, it presumably gets bigger and more powerful under parental guidance, so that by adulthood it is as substantial as the Pigpen side and is presumably adequate to control the impulse side when the horse threatens to get loose.

While we have the horse in view, it is probably important to point out that sometimes the manager-control part gets to be so overgrown that it stifles the horse's movements so that one's power is essentially hobbled.

Children are generally very resilient in resisting this kind of curb on their natural irrepressibility, but excessive restraint even at the hands of the most well-meaning adults can contribute unwittingly to the overgrowth of the control side of a child, to the detriment of the spirited accomplishment of the horse. Again, I speak here not only about children, but also about sixty-five-year-olds looking back on life, regretfully observing that their steeds never left the pasture because of overweening internal constraint, frequently much more severe and punitive than any parent ever intended it to be.

I once drew this picture for a little boy's daily caretaker, who was eagerly searching for ways to corral this irrepressible young mustang without bribing him or punishing him. As I explained with the help of the picture, the adult can augment the management-control part of the economy in a situation by supplying firm reins from the grown-up's own larger, better-developed management side without burdening the child with either bribes or punishment. For example, the grown-up could say, "Your hands are out of control here; I have to stop you," and then do whatever was necessary to do the stopping. Sometimes this would mean clasping a child's hands, hugging him, and saying, "These hands aren't for hitting. Here, we'll talk to your hands. What words do we have for your hands?"

If this intervention sounds ludicrously insufficient to stop a raring young horse, I am here to testify that I have successfully used these techniques with hospitalized, impulse-ridden children while they were attempting to hit, bite, kick, and otherwise discharge their rage onto me. I am referring to boys from ten to twelve years old, some of whom were very strong, and none of whom understood fences.

At the hospital we were taught to use what was called "tender restraint" with these raging colts. This could mean holding a child's hands firmly behind his back while saying, "This isn't good for you. I'm going to hold you right here until you can get your hands under control." It is true that in the hospital setting, in extreme circumstances, one might have to say, "I have to get us more help. You're not able to get control, and someone will have to come and help you get back to your class. We can't play more today, but we'll try it again tomorrow."

I am assuming that for most of you reading this book, the misbehavior and aggression of your children doesn't hold a candle to the impulse level I am describing. Neither did the behavior of the little boy whose caretaker wanted to check his impulses, though it is true that stopping him could be a little like stopping a bee intent on gaining his rose.

The point I want to make here is that the lesson I was teaching the nanny was not lost on the young subject himself, who at the time was five years old. He asked to see this picture and looked at the marks I had added to show how the control side gradually had to get bigger and bigger with age with the kind of help I have described. I had explained to the young woman that making herself an ally to the child's own insufficient regulator, without placing any conditions on the matter and without threats or aggression, would help him to build a stronger control side for his own impulses.

The five-year-old asked if he could take the picture with him. A week or so later, his father reported to me a remarkable scene from one of the family's more turbulent melees, when their two children were both turning bedtime into a circus, with the young colts clearly outflanking the trainers in charge. As the parents became more and more exasperated and angry at having their authority and their own rest so routed, the scene became something of a shouting match. At that point, our young hero ran out of the room and came back with the impulse-control picture he had brought home from my office.

"Wait!" he yelled. "Stop! *Everybody* here is out of control! See, we all have to get this other side to get us back into control!"

This development is of course not an ordinary one, and I am not claiming that from henceforth this family had no more bedtime circuses or other melees. Like most families, they still struggled with finding ways to corral horses without stifling them. Even if one agrees with the principle of making an ally of the child's embryonic control by augmenting it with one's adult strength in a firm but nonpunitive manner, it is not so easy to implement the idea in a moment of crisis. The difficulty is that, even if we have an entire repertoire of techniques that stem from the model of unconditional help (and I hope to offer more of them), few of us are immune to feelings of powerlessness and the inevitable accompanying feelings of anger when children are unruly, disrespectful, and generally exasperating and out of hand.

Herein lies the rub of executing this excellent paradigm of avoiding the circular-exchange way of thinking and acting. The difficulty, going back to the stick figure, is that the Pigpen side of the adult gets triggered instead of the benign grown-up control side, and then the impulse level of everyone concerned gets larger relative to the management side, and everyone gets, as the little boy said, "out of control," with no benign rescuers in sight. This difficulty brings us back to the first point of this chapter: feeling insufficient ourselves.

What usually triggers the Pigpen side of us as parents in these difficult situations is that the child's behavior seems to diminish us. Like the schoolteacher who feels personally disrespected when children do not do their homework, or the piano teacher who experiences a loss of self-regard when the student does not practice, the parent whose child does not "behave well" often feels put in a bad light, demeaned, reduced, and thus angry at the child. "I've reared a monster! What does this say about *me?*" Self-doubt, however hidden from view, is the firecracker that sets us all off. Woe unto the child who inadvertently converts this doubt into parental rage.

It is partly this ignition of the parental impulse side that makes the alliance with the child's embryonic control side so tenuous for many of us. It is what makes it hard to intervene in such a way as to align our concern, presence, and love with the part of the child that is a victim of the aggressive impulse — not against the child, as though he were synonymous with the aggression.

In the case of the little boy who was choking his young cousin at a family gathering, one can imagine that for many parents, it would be so important to attend to the needs of the attacked that the attacker's need for a benign ally would go unmet.

If the parent had sufficient presence of mind and had an interior feeling of "enoughness," and if he were convinced that this was a matter not for punishment but for another, more powerful intervention, one way to proceed would be to throw his arms around Johnny and say with concern but not accusation, "Oh, Johnny, I have to stop you! Cousins are not for hurting! Now we need some words here. If you're angry, I'll help you *tell* it. Hold on to me with those hands until we can find the words, because your hands are trying to do the talking."

In this case, trying to get at the truth of who wronged whom first and who the real bad boy is and assigning appropriate punishment to the aggressor would be the weakest kind of help that could be offered. One would not be "assisting" at all here. Indeed, the act of punishment would only build more aggression; it would fuel the Pigpen side of the young man's struggle toward self-regulation rather than the management side that the parent is trying to build.

These are a few of the illustrations of how the "beyond deserving" model is more powerful than the old manipulative one, and how it can actually be implemented.

In the next chapter we will turn our attention to that intriguing list of tasks spelled out in Dickinson's poem that fall to that growing creature who plays the *major* role in developing into the full bloom of love and work.

6. The Major Actor: The Child

Returning to our guiding poem, we notice in the third stanza a puzzle of sorts. A series of tasks to be accomplished by some unstated party is suddenly introduced, and we gradually discover that that party is a flower. It is from the standpoint of the flower that the poet is observing what goes on in a garden:

> To pack the Bud — oppose the Worm —
> Obtain its right of Dew —
> Adjust the Heat — elude the Wind —
> Escape the prowling Bee

If we were speaking only of literal flowers and their careers in a literal garden, this list of responsibilities would perhaps be self-evident. In the case of children, however, each of these intriguing metaphors raises a host of questions and allusions.

Packing the Bud: Stoking Future Potentialities

Literally speaking, what would it mean for a bud to be "packed"? I suppose it would mean that, if a plant is going to produce a bud that will in turn produce a bloom, it will be about the business of storing up chlorophyll and whatever nourishments a plant has to have to become mature enough to put forth its shoots into the light of day.

There is a memorable passage in *The Little Prince* about a rosebush preparing to produce a flower:

> But the shrub soon stopped growing, and began to get ready to produce a flower. The little prince, who was present at the first appearance of a huge bud, felt at once that some sort of miraculous apparition must emerge from it. But the flower was not satisfied to complete the preparations for her beauty in the shelter of her green chamber. She chose her colors with the greatest care. She dressed herself slowly. She adjusted her petals one by one. She did not wish to go out into the world all rumpled, like the field poppies. It was only in the full radiance of her beauty that she wished to appear. . . .[1]

In the case of a child, what is actually going on when, "in her secret chamber," a rose-to-be is packing her bud?

The Child's Active Role

What strikes us first is the fact that the rose was taking an active role on her own behalf. And so it is with a child. Even from the outset of life, the infant is not simply a passive recipient of outside ministrations.

Life begins in active protest. Infants declare volumes from the first cry. They howl and thrash and wriggle. They persevere in getting their needs felt and understood. They root for food, and they insist on their own terms, including the privilege of nay-saying.

It is true, as the very wise D. W. Winnicott once said at a scientific meeting, that "there is no such thing as an infant" — that is to say, as he went on to explain, "whenever one finds an infant, one finds maternal care" (primary care-giving), "and without maternal care there would be no infant."[2]

But it is important for parents to recognize, even from the first hours and days of life, that a child is in a significant sense an individual. The sig-

---

1. Saint-Exupéry, *The Little Prince*, English version (New York: Harcourt, Brace, 1943), p. 29.

2. D. W. Winnicott, *The Maturational Processes and the Facilitating Environment* (New York: International Universities Press, 1965), p. 39, footnote 1.

nals of this other being are present and worthy of respect; disregarding them is costly to a child's early sense of potency.

For example, a child can get the message from the outset of life that feeding is someone else's agenda. Something as apparently innocuous as jiggling the bottle to nudge the infant to take another half-ounce of milk can communicate the message that the feeding belongs to someone else, and that eating well is some kind of assignment.

The toddler and the preschooler have their own ways of claiming the active role. When a young child hugs his teddy bear, he is not only seeking comfort from the bear as a substitute for his mother; he is becoming the caring party, putting the bear in the role of the recipient. As one little boy put it, tenderly picking up his bear, "He's crying; I need to pick him up." He was experimenting with what it feels like to be the giver — that is, the active force in the giving.

Children's Play as Packing the Bud

When we see children playing, the importance of what they are doing may escape our notice. Perhaps we think that children are just amusing themselves until they are old enough to "work" and "take responsibility."

Far from being frivolous or trivial, however, children's play is work on significant issues of life. Here is where they use toys to give themselves tangible renditions of their interior strivings — their wishes, hopes, struggles, apprehensions, and fears about themselves, as well as their concerns about their parents and siblings.

In their play, children do something analogous to what we all do when we dream: we cast some unfinished problem back into the mind and wrestle with it, whether we simply restate the problem in some humorous or absurd or simply different way, or whether we try to come up with a possible solution to what is troubling us. In Chapter 5 we noted how Wordsworth saw the seriousness in the play of a child. He was not alone in this insight.

It was a momentous day when Sigmund Freud thoughtfully noticed his grandson playing with a toy, making it disappear and then reappear, saying "Gone!" in the first place, then "There!" in the second. Was he "just playing"? What Freud observed was that the child was about the business of mastering something. He was coming to terms with his mother's absence.[3]

This observation was a seed to our understanding better the natural urge of children to give tangible form to their pressing subjective concerns. Their play is the way they begin to take responsibility for those concerns, working on them, so to speak, with toys onto which they can project these internal matters in order to wrestle with them more effectively.

Freud's observation was also the seed from which sprang the idea of play therapy for children when subjective concerns become so acute that they threaten to overwhelm them. In this kind of therapy, we make a safe place — a safe relationship — in which this natural urge of children to give tangible form to pressing subjective concerns can be maximized when, finding life's tasks too formidable, they need an assistant.

Each line of Dickinson's poem throws light on an aspect of the child's "work," whether it is done alone, with siblings and parents, or with a mentor, teacher, or therapist.

Opposing the Worm: Wrestling with Gnawing Conflicts

Various concerns, conflicts, fears, and worries simply arise in the process of growing up. These are normal experiences in the lives of all children; all of us will experience some degree of inner discord. In my reading of the guiding poem, the image of a gnawing worm alludes to all such interference — static on the line, so to speak, that can sometimes occupy a child's mind almost to the exclusion of other important matters. Schoolwork, for example, can suffer when a child involuntarily "zones out" and becomes preoccupied with what he senses to be more urgent than what the teacher has in mind.

But how could this struggle, if all of us are heir to it — if it is simply a part of the natural course of human development — create such a state of conflict in a child's mind that it would amount to being gnawed at inside?

We note, in the first place, that *wishing* for the unimpeded gratification of all desires and appetites is inescapable, as is the necessity of restraining the appetites and enduring the frustration of our wishes.

3. Sigmund Freud, *Beyond the Pleasure Principle*, standard edition, 18 (London: Hogarth Press, 1955), pp. 14-15.

In the heyday of the Freudian discoveries about impulse and restraint, some thought that the parent's task was to avoid getting in the way of all impulses, thus eliminating guilt and conflict. Children then would grow up well-adjusted and happy!

But things did not prove to be so simple. The sad discovery was that without restraint, children themselves (not to mention their siblings and parents) suffered other kinds of woes. In other words, the undercontrol of impulses proved as troublesome as the overcontrol of impulses. No child is more persecuted internally than one who feels that no one is bigger than his impulses, because he feels abandoned to those impulses. Might he then overrun his parents and the whole world? Guilt feelings again reign supreme; they may be even more destructive than the guilt feelings associated with the "overcontrol" school of thought, in which "children should be seen and not heard."

If conflict, then, is part of the natural state of the human being, how can we come to understand better the conflict itself?

Echoes from Literature

If we need any substantiation of this gnawing worm beyond our observations of ourselves, our children, and the morning newspaper, we might pause here and listen to a few echoes from the chorus of our great writers, who long before Freud spoke tellingly of the struggle within the human mind. Many of them — Greeks, early Hebrews, noble Romans — spoke to this ubiquitous theme of *agon,* or struggle, for dealing with that theme is very often what makes literature endure. Here we consider a few glimpses from writers who make this fact altogether palpable.

To start with a challenging example, William Blake uses the very metaphor under discussion — that of a worm eating a flower:

O Rose, thou art sick.
The invisible worm,
That flies in the night,
In the howling storm,

Has found out thy bed
Of crimson joy:

> And his dark secret love
> Does thy life destroy.[4]

Like Dickinson, Blake knows that all is not well in nature's literal garden. And, like her, he is referring at a deep level to human beings who are being attacked at the core.

From children's books about where the wild things dwell, to the games that lure the young away from all the worthwhile endeavors adults want them to engage in, to the movies that mesmerize, however temporarily, the world at large, one does not travel far in any direction without encountering the war between desire and impulse on the one hand and the manacles of absolute restraint on the other.

We can see, for example, that the young child moves quickly from the paradise of infancy, where what he wants is accepted almost always as what he needs, to the inevitable sphere of war between appetites and their frustration. Wishes begin to conflict with the requirements of civilization, to bring Freud's formulation into it.

Wordsworth said it this way:

> Heaven lies about us in our infancy!
> Shades of the prison-house begin to close
>   Upon the growing Boy. . . .

and

> Thou little Child, yet glorious in the might
> Of heaven-born freedom on thy being's height,
> Why with such earnest pains dost thou provoke
> The years to bring the inevitable yoke,
> Thus blindly with thy blessedness at strife?
> Full soon thy Soul shall have her earthly freight,
> And custom lie upon thee with a weight,
> Heavy as frost, and deep almost as life![5]

4. William Blake, *The Poetry and Prose of William Blake,* ed. D. V. Erdman (New York: Doubleday, 1988), p. 23.

5. William Wordsworth, "Ode: Intimations of Immortality from Recollections of Early Childhood," in *The Selected Poetry and Prose of Wordsworth,* ed. G. Hartman (New York: Meridian, 1980), p. 167.

In *Moby Dick,* which I quoted in another connection in Chapter 5, Melville portrays in Ahab's tormented compulsion for revenge against his dismemberer a distillation of human internal suffering that evokes in his readers a recognition of some unavoidable reality that no human being can escape. That is to say, that good and evil war within us, that we are subject to forces not of our own making and not ultimately under our control, and that struggling with these forces is our human lot.

Dickinson says all of the above, and a great deal of what the children in Part I have shown to us, in eight short lines:

> The mob within the heart
> Police cannot suppress
> The riot given at the first
> Is authorized as peace
>
> Uncertified of scene
> Or signified of sound
> But growing like a hurricane
> In a congenial ground.

Dickinson, #1745

I end this section by noting that this unceasing disharmony is not in itself useless. For example, the degrees of aggression that reside in all of us, "the keen teeth of the fierce tiger's jaw" (Shakespeare, Sonnet #19), can scarcely be separated from the vital strivings that make us human. For one thing, they are an important ingredient of our sexual nature, without which life would be "carved and cool" — to quote Dickinson again — and laid in stone (as well as eventually nonexistent!). There is an essential vitality that Dickinson aptly described:

> . . . I had a sort that moved —
> A Sense that smote and stirred —
> Instincts for Dance — a caper part —
> An Aptitude for Bird —

Dickinson, #1046

Dickinson ends this poem with a declaration that the human reach toward Being and Motion and Breath — through centuries to come — will not end.

Obtaining the Right of Dew: Procuring Nourishment

From birth, children have a sense of the nourishment they need. In observing their play, we see many of them spontaneously drawing two overlapping hills, with a sun shining over all, and often with a stream of water running underneath. Is that not a hearkening back to the paradise of the "good breast," in whatever form and to whatever degree a child experienced it? That is, with every new life, there is a fountain of dew present from the outset through the caring presence of the parental figure, who provides not only physical nourishment but the warmth, the holding, the brimming-over affection for this new creature. But of course the nourishment can be insufficient. (The tragic, total, fatal failure of all early dew for the infant constitutes a subject for a different book.)

Images crowd in from the sea of little children who in different ways have appealed to me for restitution and replenishment of the insufficient dew of their early weeks and months of life. One little girl, after two or three play sessions, drew a picture of a cat turning her back on a bowl of milk. Around the entire picture the girl painted a black frame. Shortly afterward, she said she did not want to come to the playroom anymore. Apparently something about the connection with me was depressing her instead of nourishing her. Perhaps, in the deep wisdom of childhood, she knew she could not get from me what actually had to come from her own mother and father, and the hungry kitten inside her turned away sorrowfully from any reminder of that truth.

Another child drew a picture of apple trees — which, not accidentally, replicated in number the members of her family. She drew apples only on the big trees, explaining that there were not any apples for the little trees.

Jennie, who has told us her story in some detail, produced an entire series of play scenes and pictures about obtaining water for birds and warm bread for her dolls. At one point she became fascinated with creating fountains, with all their implications of plenitude.

One little boy said of his protagonist, "He lives in a desert, so he has to scratch out a little water by digging deep down into the sand." Another young boy had very good but very busy parents. Because the dew he craved was something that he simply could not get in sufficient amounts from his mother and father, he resorted to trying to find it by sucking on his clothes (an attempt to slake his thirst that is not unusual). More important, in the treatment room he discovered a rewarding piece of play for himself. With the play dough I had given him, he would make cookies for a toy horse and generously feed him. Then he would mount the horse and gleefully "ride" it through the office, announcing that now that his horse had had enough cookies to eat, it could take him *anywhere* he wanted to go.

Nearly all the young children who have ever had a course of therapy in my playroom have been drawn from the outset to this play dough. Indeed, when I worked years ago in a children's hospital, which housed impoverished patients who were there mainly because of the insufficiency of the early dew, I discovered that this play dough (which I made myself from flour, salt, and warm water) had an extraordinary appeal. It had such an appeal, in fact, that I began to ponder what this dough was providing for these children that was different from the other play materials in the room. Let me tell the story of one of these children, whom I will call William.

William — whom we met briefly in the previous chapter — announced early on that what he was good at was "hitting people in the face." I was not surprised to see that the burden of his therapeutic work — far more weighty than his academic bankruptcy — had to do with an explosive rage that alternated between this task he was "good at" and a tight-lipped refusal to participate in anything that was happening in the classroom.

He often seemed quite withdrawn, and he stored up grudges against his classmates, only to explode in an assaultive attack at some minor offense on the playground. Unable to give or receive friendly feelings toward the other children, and hostile toward all adults, he attached himself to an older boy who reigned as chief aggressor on the playground. This boy gave William the assignment of instigating fights with newcomers and smaller children.

In the play therapy room, one could see immediately the same picture: a cautious, silent constriction alternating with erratic demonstrations of anger. Sometimes William would set out little men facing a lineup of cars, and one by one he would "fire" the cars at the men, methodically "mowing them down." If there were any survivors, William would call in the larger Batman car, which would then complete the massacre. One would not immediately associate William, the "masculine" menace, with a warm, soft, and pliable material. He was a hardened young man of violent action.

However, in one of William's early play sessions, his eye fell on the dough, which lay on the doll table, and he picked it up and began to play with it. He squeezed it, patted it, cut it into tiny pieces, and made a big pile of the pieces on one side of the table. The next play session began and ended in the same way, and for some weeks William concerned himself almost exclusively with this material. He asked whether he might help me make the dough, and each time we would have a little ceremony of mixing the salt and flour with the warm water and stirring it and kneading it until it had the right consistency. His original reticence about coming to sessions gave way to unbridled enthusiasm. He asked why he could not come every day. Something about that dough was making a powerful connection with him.

One day William thoughtfully pushed a piece of the dough into a tiny plastic cup, made a deep hole in it with his finger, and asked me whether I would keep it for him until it was dry. About the same time, this "macho" youngster began to express interest in a baby doll. At each session he picked up the nursing bottle to feed her, sometimes asking me if I would hold the baby and rock it for him. One day, long after I thought he had forgotten the dough-filled plastic cup, he asked for it and decided to take it with him when he left. His teacher told me that in class he often removed this strange little toy from his desk and appeared to drink from it. Clearly he had devised a way to take this symbolic nourishment with him into the larger world.

What William was addressing here was the business of "obtaining his right of dew." (If readers are interested in hearing more about his odyssey in play therapy, they can read about it in *The Man in the Yellow Hat*.[6]) For our present purposes, his story provides an example of how readily children will seize an opportunity to exercise their right of dew.

Returning for a moment to the metaphor of the plant: A plant reminds us that the children are in the morning part of life. If a plant gets dew in the morning, it can draw on it during the heat of the day. A great deal of the dew that seems necessary for human beings to survive does seem to be given in infancy and early childhood through the caring presence of parents. However, if youngsters are accidentally deprived of adequate dew in the morning of very early childhood, they can partially obtain it in later benevolent influences: teachers, the school, the church or synagogue, the wider caring community, not to mention the entire world of the arts, especially books.

6. Dorothy W. Martyn, *The Man in the Yellow Hat* (Atlanta: Scholars Press, 1992), pp. 25-50.

Here the children I worked with in the hospital have something to tell us. These were children who certainly had not been read to, for their parents had simply not known what Dickinson referred to as "those kinsmen of the shelf," who "enamor in prospective, and satisfy — obtained," who provide "bells within," though it may be "wilderness without" (Dickinson, #604). Hence my surprise when these children, ranging in age from seven to about twelve, so long deprived of the birthright of being read to by a loving parent, were drawn to a blanket where I sat on the floor with a few books, waiting to see if any child would approach and ask for a story.

Any child? It was as though they were little chickens, and I had spread out corn. They were ravenously hungry to be fed from these books! To my astonishment, the fairy tales I read to them — with some skepticism that the vocabulary would be accessible to them — were so engaging that one young boy, after hearing "Hansel and Gretel" for the first time, put the book into his mouth and literally tried to eat it.

The poet who will not stay out of these pages had more to say about books and their thirst-quenching properties:

Strong Draughts of Their Refreshing minds
To drink — enables Mine
Through Desert of the Wilderness
As bore it Sealed Wine —

To go elastic — Or as One
The Camel's trait — attained —
How powerful the Stimulus
Of an Hermetic Mind —

Dickinson, #711

This poem speaks of a heady, grown-up kind of wine, which may seem far removed from the needs of childhood, but it is simply another kind of the dew about which we are speaking. In infancy, such draughts come from the "good breast," in all of its literal and symbolic manifestations. It is this morning dew with which we are mainly concerned here, that fountain flowing from parents and other mentors who have been given the gift to love children, primarily from parents who were also given the gift to be able to love.

Adjusting the Heat: Managing Anger and Sexual Strivings

When I try to think about what this "heat" is that somehow needs "adjusting" for a plant — or a child — to thrive, I look to the children first to inform me.

When I reread the poet's reference to a flower's adjusting the heat, what flashes first into my mind is one of those pictures painted by Jennie, that paragon of a child utterly intent on pleasing adults. It depicts a red monster looming over an entire sheet of drawing paper and carries the dubious caption "I luv you." I think also of her picture with flaming fireworks and the words "Bang!" and "Rip!" All this heat beneath the surface brings to mind another of Dickinson's poems, the one about a volcano covered on its exterior by a peaceful scene:

> On my volcano grows the Grass
> A meditative spot —
> An acre for a Bird to choose
> Would be the General thought —
>
> How red the Fire rocks below —
> How insecure the sod
> Did I disclose. . . .

Dickinson, excerpt from #1677

The bad feelings hinted at in Jennie's pictures are in some children — and not just in hospitalized children — sometimes amplified into truly harrowing scenes that they play out with toys. Little boys lean toward creating horrific wars where bad guys get hacked to pieces, burned up in fires, cannibalized on occasion, or blown to smithereens. Since these atrocities are given expression by boys who are actually experiencing only the mildest of symptoms — for example, "can't concentrate on math" — we have to assume that these matters of heat are not very limited in their distribution.

The children I knew in the hospital, all of whom, like William, had been grossly and unintentionally deprived of their "right of dew," often turned this heat loose on the world around them, unleashing destructive rage on whatever target was at hand. I have known at least two little girls with such a level of rage that their rampages would require all the ingenuity and firmness of the adult in charge to stop them. I can see them now. One would try to tear books off shelves, to flood the playroom with water from the sink, to attack the therapist with teeth, feet, and fists. The other, in the midst of an apparently happy tea party for the dolls, suddenly erupted into a fury, turning over the toy tea table and knocking all its contents, including the dolls, onto the floor. "She has a spell on her," she said of one of the dolls.

Both little girls remind me of Dickinson's further apt words about volcanoes. She speaks of them in terms of "smouldering anguish," which

> . . .
>
> Bear within — appalling Ordnance,
> Fire, and smoke, and gun,
> Taking Villages
> Taking Villages for breakfast,
> And appalling Men — . . . .

Dickinson, excerpt from #175

How do children learn to adjust such heat? We begin by recognizing that emotional heat seems to come onstage with the human organism: the infant protests vigorously at birth, and this protest is welcomed as the first sign of health. Next comes the infant's raging and flailing in his crib until his needs are met, and new versions of "heat" continue throughout life.

Clearly, the heat at first gets adjusted by the parents, for an infant has no built-in means of adjusting it. The first help arrives when the parents willingly, even gladly, take on this task by offering comfort and a loving presence to contain the troublesome feelings.

The child's ability to take on this task himself grows out of the parents' facility both in managing their own internal heat and in extending benign help to the child (see Chapter 5). The parents enable the child to feel understood in his hot anger, thus teaching him through tender restraint, and by example, to contain such strong feelings. Anthony, Jennie, and Henry demonstrated for us the ability to modify their combustible material within a relationship wherein they could find the kind of assistance they needed.

Another part of that parental help can come when mother or father reads fairy tales to the child. We are reminded of the affinity children have for *Where the Wild Things Are,* so immortally rendered by Maurice

Sendak.[7] Similarly, there is the universal appeal to children of fairy tales where bad wolves meet their end in boiling water; where the witch gets burned up in the stove after threatening to cook the children and eat them; where the hero barely escapes the wrath of the giant in the attic.

These scary figures tell children something about themselves — that is, about their own bad feelings that won't stay underground, however hard they try to bury them. These bad feelings are mainly angry feelings, and every child feels some relief to discover from a story that the scary things do not win the day. For children, who are not consciously aware that these scary creatures represent their own bad feelings, nevertheless feel reassured that their own anger cannot destroy the world. That is an essential step in emotional growth, and it can be learned both from the parents as involved models and from the immortal literature of fairy tales, as well as from their sequels in the literature of the ages.

Eluding the Wind: Coping with Internal and External Pressures

We return first to the rose in *The Little Prince*. Before presenting herself to the world, she had something to say about the wind, one of the possible threats she faced on the new planet where she found herself: "I am not afraid of tigers, but I have a horror of drafts of wind. Have you no windshield here?"[8]

Of course we do not want our young to be fearful of every wind that comes along. Without some exposure to outside forces, some gentle breezes, so to speak, children would have no opportunity to build up strength against the stronger winds they must endure later on. But how do they best build up that needed strength? With that question in mind, we begin by noting that there are two kinds of threatening winds. One kind blows from without; the other blows from within.

On a literal level, "The Three Little Pigs" is about a dangerous wind coming from outside the self. This captivating story has presented to generations of children one of their first suspense-filled literary adventures, offering sound advice on protection from being blown down by adverse winds. In the story there is a big bad wolf, and who does not remember

7. Maurice Sendak, *Where the Wild Things Are* (New York: HarperCollins, 1964).
8. Saint-Exupéry, *The Little Prince*, pp. 30-31.

trembling under his terrifying howl: "I'll huff and I'll puff, and I'll blow your house down!"

And there are, of course, literal dangers that come at us from outside ourselves. We can even sense the literal level in a Dickinson poem:

Down Time's quaint stream
Without an oar
We are enforced to sail
Our Port a secret
Our Perchance a Gale
What Skipper would
Incur the Risk
What Buccaneer would ride
Without a surety from the Wind
Or schedule of the Tide-

Dickinson, #1656

Outside winds that are too cold, too strong, or too overwhelming can threaten to chill or snap the young being's stem. They produce the tragedies in our society: war, poverty, drugs — all the ills that blow cruelly on the young who have inadequate protection. These are winds that cannot be successfully — or at least easily — eluded.

Almost all of the children I knew at the hospital had endured and were enduring the bitter wind and sleet that blow on those who have no real place in our society of plenty. Most of these children were being brought up by mothers and grandmothers in the absence of fathers who, despairing of being able to meet the family's needs, had left. The remaining female parents had scarce material possessions and were themselves so blown about by adversity that they could provide little protection for their young. Winds that chill the parents must inevitably affect their little ones.

But there are also winds of less than hurricane force that can threaten the thriving of the young: winds of discord between the parents; old winds that have been blowing toxic fumes around in a given family for generations; winds of financial adversity. There are the winds of fortune and, in some homes, the "winds of doctrine" that can whip around and hurt. There are winds that come briefly, like a family storm that "blows over," and there are air currents that blow steadily, like the trade winds. Learning to stand up in the wind, or learning to hide from the wind, or learning other means to sustain oneself in the inevitable squalls, gales, and tempests of human existence is "intricately done," as our guiding poem puts it, and will require help from those of us who modestly assist.

We recall that Anthony once expressed his fears about the financial pressures his parents were feeling, and their attempts to confront them, by drawing a picture of a windstorm that was raining computers.

Some children experience the winds of discord between their parents as thunderstorms, if not hurricanes. Sometimes a crisis in the parental relationship can throw children into such difficulties with their schoolwork that their academic boats capsize. When the parents' boat starts to right itself, the steadying of the children's own craft usually follows suit. The children's learning to elude the wind is assisted or impeded by how the parents themselves manage winds, as well as whether the parents stand with the children or add to the wind by standing over against them.

The "winds of doctrine," by which I mean religious or other ideological pressures unrelentingly applied in the home, have strained — if not buckled — the underpinnings of more than one child in my acquaintance. In the play therapy of one very troubled young boy, I remember the appearance of a besieged protagonist who faced destruction by an enemy. When I noted the dire situation that the hero found himself in, the child commented, "You see, they are going to sacrifice him to their gods."

The strict enforcement of severe rules, erroneously thought to make children "well behaved," even including the coercion and punishment sometimes still taught and advocated by certain religious groups, has done enormous damage to the well-being of more than one of my patients. Somewhat similarly, a parental injunction stemming from a well-meaning attempt to inculcate honesty in a child can so hard-wire the child's mind that he has to subject every utterance to close and intimidating scrutiny before proceeding with any attempted communication. This can make it difficult for a child to finish sentences without running into a blank wall of hesitance.

We return to the story of "The Three Little Pigs," reading it now as symbolic poetry. Children who hear this early nursery tale are of course not aware that it is as riveting as it is because, like all great literature, it tells them something about their own inner make-up. It tells them about the long process of becoming stronger *inside* relative to their own strong feelings. It powerfully addresses the inner conflict between impulse and self-regulation that I spelled out in the previous chapter via my teaching tool of the stick figure. The story is doubly compelling because it is poetry about the menace children experience from their own angry feelings that threaten to devour them.

Anthony, Jennie, and Henry gave us many a view of troublesome winds that blew upon them from the outside, as well as the internal tempests they were learning to struggle with better. They also used the image of the wind in very positive ways as well as negative ones. When Jennie designed her last house in the playroom, the houseboat in which she prepared to launch out on her own beyond play therapy, one of her main concerns was to make sails that would catch the wind. She mentioned that the power had to come from the wind, and she wanted to harness it.

Henry, whose odyssey also led him to the image of a boat, gave us two intriguing lines about wind: In making the mast for his ship, he remarked that "It would have to hold everything up," especially the sails, "which would catch the wind and give the ship power." However, in deciding on the length of rope needed to "pull the craft up onto the beach," he said it was important not to make the rope too short, "because if a strong wind came while the boat was anchored, the wind would blow the ship over." While making sure that his Viking ship had provisions for using the power of the wind, he inadvertently echoed a line in one of Dickinson's poems: "the life that is tied too tight escapes" (#1535). That idea of too short a rope, as regards children, is perhaps a more concise rendering of much of what I said in Chapter 5 about the difference between "assisting" and "controlling" a young creature.

What does protect the young child from being blown over by the wind? What is for children the equivalent of the "windshield" requested by the Little Prince's rose? One detail not mentioned previously about Jennie's last boat, the one for self-launching, was her surprising request for "one of those plastic things that holds bottles of Coke together." When I supplied one, I watched with fascination to see what she intended to do with it. She placed it over the entire boat, remarking that the boat needed a partial shelter over it. But this "plastic thing" also had its own holes. The boat, you see, needed not only shelter but also plenty of open space for air to get through. What wisdom children have! They learn, and we learn through them, that they need both protection and the growth that comes from managing their own winds.

Escaping the Prowling Bee: Contending with Overweening Conscience and "Meddling" Adults

It is at first puzzling that Dickinson completed her list of tasks for a flower with that of escaping "the prowling bee." She was a consummate gardener who not only knew very well that bees pollinate flowers but also knew that, from antiquity, the bee has represented the poet's muse. She wrote many a "buzzing" poem with this double reference clearly just under the surface. The bee's intrusion into and intimacy with the flower presented her with many an opportunity to tease pious Amherst a bit with their overt sexual allusions while clearly referring also to the bee as muse, fertilizing her own creativity. Here is one of the most mischievous of these poems, which concludes with one of her profound references to herself as a poet:

> A Bee his burnished Carriage
> Drove boldly to a Rose —
> Combinedly alighting —
> Himself — his Carriage was —
> The Rose received his visit
> With frank tranquillity
> Withholding not a Crescent
> To his Cupidity —
> Their Moment consummated —
> Remained for him — to flee —
> Remained for her — of rapture
> But the humility.

Dickinson, #1339

This bee certainly was not something to escape!

That the intrusive role of bees, as well as the intrusive role of parents, is necessary to the pollinization and the fructification of living things is of course obvious and indisputable. A very memorable and appealing way of describing these necessary efforts on the part of parents was given to us by Selma Fraiburg in her timeless and wise book for parents entitled *The Magic Years*. After she described in detail the earliest gratifying and nurturing era of infancy, she entitled a chapter "The Missionaries Arrive."[9]

9. Selma Fraiburg, *The Magic Years* (New York: Scribner, 1959).

The "intricate affair" we are discussing, that of preparing young human flowers to be offered as "butterflies to the meridian," inevitably involves certain civilizing influences that the young do not request. They have to be "carefully taught," as one songwriter put it. Some things do not come naturally. Brushing teeth, washing hands, hanging up coats, and chewing with mouths closed would be included among a few hundred items that in the language of the experts come under the heading of "socialization." Children need parents or other role models to teach them these things, even if they would prefer not to be intruded upon by such requirements. Not surprisingly, all children sometimes have the impulse to escape such a "prowling bee."

The Sting of the Bee

I knew one little girl, about six years old, and an even younger little boy, perhaps three years old, who literally tried to climb out of windows to escape the presence of their parents. Apparently there was some interference or sting they felt to be imminent that urged them to flee.

Taking for granted the altogether well-intended efforts of the good parents of both these children, the question presents itself: What part of this parental care seemed to these loved children so terribly intrusive? Numerous children have taught me that what they run from is, paradoxically, often intended to help them with something they actually want very much themselves — namely, to learn, to thrive, to grow stronger, and to reach for the sun.

I have yet to meet a child who did not aspire to excellence in some sense, even though all that might seem possible was to get better at "hitting people in the face," as young William put it. This strong internal signal to press for excellence is in fact hard to silence. What can drown it out, however, is a parent's or a teacher's own agenda for the child, insistently put forward, either overtly or covertly.

Learning to read is a good example. Most children who have been graced by parents who read to them and who enjoy that experience want to learn to read for themselves. Stories and books as undemanding friends attract children as predictably as pollen attracts bees or corn attracts chickens. But well-meaning adults, eager to "make their children smarter," as I noted on the cover of a parents magazine recently, can inadvertently stifle this natural propensity by buzzing around the child's head with intrusive signals to hurry up and learn. Escaping this buzz can then become more important than learning to read.

Sometimes adults can become so directive that the child's natural urge to reach toward the sun is thoroughly and virtually permanently stifled. I have had patients who, as adults, have spent precious years unconsciously halting their own growth in order to run from the feeling of being at the mercy of someone else's direction. It can become so paramount to escape the long-internalized sting of another's domination that one can literally feel more alive in resisting authority than in discovering and pursuing one's own aspirations.

Do you know anyone who is consistently critical and finding fault with others? You are almost certainly looking at a grown-up who, as a child, was stung by criticism. We inevitably grow up swallowing the parental voice, and it can become our own. If that voice was critical, the most likely result is that we arrive at adulthood criticizing both ourselves and others.

The Killer Bee

There are fairly big bees out there in a world with other people in it, but, as we have seen, the killer bees are mostly the ones within. These internal bees have very large antennae. Children see and hear and feel in megadecibels. That angry look on a parent's face is for the child a beloved grandmother turning into a wolf. And those angry feelings a child may have experienced during the day turn into monsters during the night. That roaring voice of the giant in the attic, who turns up quite often in this book, grows even louder when that voice becomes the child's own internal voice. It can turn a slight external criticism into "I must be really, really bad." In the playroom, one little boy made his dungeon for bad guys in layers, the bottom one being "where the *really* bad ones go."

The feeling of being somehow deficient in a parent's eyes can live right on for years in the form of being vulnerable to the slightest hint from without that we are not worth very much. The current slang word for this sting is being "dissed." Another version is being "lessed." This experience of being disregarded or not considered, *amplified within* becomes "I must be very disregardable," followed by anger at the agent through whom the message has come.

The same sequence ensues in the experience of feeling truly unloved. The distance between "I do not feel loved" and "I must not be lovable" is very short. It is the belittled place within that is so subject to being stung. It inclines a child — and most of the rest of us — to flee the bee of possible disapproval, the sting of feeling like a bad, disappointing child. Dickinson speaks often about this sting within:

My Soul — accused me — And I quailed —
As Tongues of Diamond had reviled. . . .

> Dickinson, #753

Ourself behind ourself, concealed —
Should startle most —

. . .

> Dickinson, #670

That she forgot me was the least
I felt it second pain
That I was worthy to forget
Was most I thought upon.

> Dickinson, #1683

"Escaping the prowling bee" in the way we are using the image has, I believe, its most helpful relevance at this point. Learning to live with a biting, stinging internal voice of self-criticism is — if I had to pick one — one of the most difficult tasks children have to master, and it is a task that has to be addressed throughout life.

So Where Is the Honey?

Fortunately, there is a use for all these bees. In fact, we could not do well without them. Tamed somewhat, they can provide us with a necessary monitoring presence that can help teach us how to manage ourselves, how to get our work done, how to love more effectively, and which way we need to travel.

Did you ever meet someone who apparently had no self-monitoring capacity at all? Those children at the hospital give us examples. Largely deprived of parental oversight and effective love, they were left to the mercy of their own impulses, and those impulses were not merciful! Without some kind of parenting that can benignly assist the young to manage the bees that come their way, how can they possibly develop within themselves an effective self-regulator?

The elusive goal, then, is to enable our children, as well as ourselves, to live with a gentle internal monitor, some creature perhaps like Jiminy Cricket, instead of a ferocious stinging bee that hurts and punishes.

How Does One Escape Prowling Bees?

There are ways of trying to escape prowling bees that are very harmful. Dickinson once said in a letter, "In all the circumference of Expression, those guileless words of Adam and Eve never were surpassed, 'I was afraid and hid myself'" (Letter #946).

Similar expressions are disturbingly common in the treatment room: "I can't seem to find my place in the world of work. Nothing lasts for me." "I simply can't finish my degree. I've had the course work done for years, but the dissertation just doesn't get finished." "I can't seem to sustain a close relationship; within a few months the flame goes out of it, and we part ways." Hiding from the prowling bees within us simply does not work.

Another attempted solution is to depend on others to give oneself enough affirmation and praise to overcome the self-criticism and self-doubt. This is a futile and self-destructive means of trying to escape. It builds anger in both the depender and the one depended on to supply the supports to hold up the fragile self.

The better way to escape the killer bees, those merciless stingers we add to the hive ourselves, is to learn to live with them — as a skilled beekeeper does — by strengthening the part of the self that can sustain and nourish self-regard. Dickinson gets at this ability when she writes about a camel's capacity to store up water for a desert crossing:

> To go elastic — Or as One
> The Camel's trait — attained —
>
> Dickinson, excerpt from #711

The question that follows immediately is, "How does one acquire that strength?" We surely know already that supplying our own water for a trip, rather than depending on the sustenance of others, is preferable. But how do we do this?

As we discussed at the end of the chapter on the family, the source of the water is conditionless love. And for those of us who are believers, the "droughtless well" that Dickinson spoke of would have to come from divine love.

However, love of the kind that is the theme of this book is not limited to families of an avowed religious faith, nor is it always plentiful in the families who do confess such a faith. There is a mystery here. If "God is love" (1 John 4:8) and "The Spirit blows where it chooses" (John 3:8, NRSV), then would it not follow that love blows where it chooses and is not the property of any of us?

What we do know is that the ability to replenish one's own supplies, and thus to escape one's bees, is more readily attained if one has had plenty of water supplied by the original loving gardeners early in life. And yet, although the three children who have given us the poetry of their play were all loved children, they still had to work very hard on both obtaining dew and escaping bees.

We can see, then, that we are speaking of both the responsibility of the assistant and the responsibility of the child in the "bright affair" of growing up. The issue of responsibility will be the primary focus of the last chapter.

7. The Snake in the Garden

The Immortality of the Snake in the Garden

Earlier I promised to come back to that old story about a snake that once upon a time showed up in a garden and caused a lot of trouble. It would seem that once upon a time is more than once upon a time; the story of the snake has a way of continuing. In fact, that reptile keeps showing up somehow in every generation in every family. Personally, professionally, and socially, I have yet to meet any family totally free from that snake that comes into our present from former generations.

To go back to the scene in the Garden of Eden, the most famous crime-and-punishment story of our culture, we note that the snake was found to be the instigator "Of Man's first disobedience, and the Fruit/Of that Forbidden Tree, whose mortal taste/Brought Death into the World, and all our woe . . ." (Milton, *Paradise Lost*, 1.11.1-3). The serpent was then "cursed above all cattle, and above every beast of the field," and was condemned to crawl on its belly and eat dust. Adam and Eve were sentenced to everlasting sorrow (Gen. 3:14-17, KJV).

Children seem to have an innate sense about this association of snakes with what is "bad" and troublesome. We may remember that Jennie, in the midst of her varying images of fierce, aggressive, threatening figures — monsters, alligators, dragons — drew a huge snake that bulged out from recently swallowed prey. She commented, "It's a bad snake; it could kill us, you know."

The multivalent imagery of the snake, which includes the phallic and sexual in its condensed allusions, does not preclude the present emphasis on its symbolizing the introduction of evil into the human scene. One does not have to subscribe to the concept of original sin to observe that there is a staggering monotony in the human story, which, with innumerable variations, endlessly re-enacts this drama of a "thief ingredient" in the happiness of all living beings, to borrow a phrase from one of Dickinson's letters (#359).

How Do We Recognize the Fellow?

If the monotonous repetition of this enemy's presence seems to be inevitable, how do we recognize the invader when we see it? At least one sign of the poisonous reptile's presence lies in the appearance of one of its primary companions: blame. When something goes awry in human affairs, the primordial feeling that someone must be blamed is almost always present. Finding out who is culpable becomes the urgent matter at hand when hurt and anger and suffering appear. It can be a chief preoccupation in families. As a homely example, if pieces of broken glass are found on the bathroom floor, the first question that finds voice in an angry parent is, "Who dropped the glass in the bathroom?" When spouses quarrel, the pressing question arises, "Who is at fault?"

At least as far back as Sophocles in the Greek tradition, searching out the one to be blamed has been seen as paramount to the health of the city. The entire tragedy of *Oedipus Rex* centered on the necessity of finding out who had brought the plague on the city by some wrongdoing. If the perpetrator could be found, that man could be punished and cast out, and the city could be saved.

In the Hebrew tradition, blame for the trouble in the original garden is famous. Questioned by the Lord God about his disobedience, Adam replied, "The woman whom thou gavest to be with me, she gave me of the tree, and I did eat." The woman, when called to account, responded, "The serpent beguiled me, and I did eat." (See Genesis 3:12-13, KJV.) From the outset of all of our troubles, it seemed necessary to find who was at fault, and the finger, according to the story, got pointed in the final analysis at this snake.

Where Does the Snake Hide?

Perhaps the cleverest guise of the intruding snake is that of its hiding under the guise of conscience, something we see in adults — indeed, in ourselves personally — as much as in children. The children and adults in my office who are looking for peace of mind are very frequently suffering under the accusatory finger of overly severe conscience. The sense of judgment of the self, apparently emanating from others, often finds its most sadistic expression in the unconscious inner voice that agrees with the external judgment.

To be sure, there are external hells in our world, such as systemic social evils and the vicious dogs of war. Here, however, we are speaking not of the external rages that attack us but of an internal suffering that lies most cruelly within our own breast.

Could such a personal hell have any relevance for the shocking murders of schoolchildren by other classmates, or for the random killings of utter strangers in some apparently senseless rampage of a lone gunman? The extra fuel for rage sufficient for killing other human beings may well be provided by our internal judgments, echoing and greatly amplifying voices from outside us that tell us we are worthless.

Our newspapers tell stories of tragic, murderous rage unloosed by some on others who they feel to be more highly valued than themselves. From the original fratricide in Genesis on down to our own times, such rage is different only in degree from the anger we all feel when some self-doubt is confirmed by an external source. When did you yourself feel really, really angry? If disregard, criticism, or another message of devaluation had something to do with it, might there have been an internal fifth column that amplified the feeling by an unconscious alliance with it? Do we ourselves participate in a belittling experience by adding a self-persecutory doubt about our worthiness? Dickinson offered this incisive comment:

> Lest I should insufficient prove . . . [is]
> The Chiefest Apprehension / Upon my thronging Mind —
> Dickinson, #751

This persecutory presence can haunt all of us from time to time with some form of self-doubt triggered by the sting of devaluation from without. It is perhaps the cleverest work of this snake. Recall little Susie from Chapter 4: her inability to sleep through the night for months on end would seem to be traceable to her feeling inside like a criminal who deserved capital punishment. She re-enacted this internal accusation with the inevitable self-punishment over and over in the presence of her mother and me until she discovered through the accepting presence of these two mother figures that she was not bad.

I have yet to meet a little boy in my playroom, brought to me most frequently because of academic problems, who has not revealed, as soon as he feels safe from judgment, that he is suffering under an inner sentence of "guilty" relative to a parent figure. In uncannily similar self-created dramas, they use little action figures to re-enact some crime against a loved (and hated) authority figure and the inevitability of severe retribution, usually capital punishment.

We remember young Anthony, so absorbed in the debilitating effects of such a conflict that he could not "pay attention" in school. He played out this story again and again, with ever-increasing determination to rob a bank, and with ever-increasing terror that the police would win out and punish him.

In Chapter 5 we spoke about how that giant in "Jack and the Beanstalk" can roar at parents as well as children. Recall how Jack repeatedly robbed the giant of his most treasured possessions and repeatedly fled threats of pending retribution. "I'll grind your bones to make my bread!" still reverberates through all generations of children who experience guilt over coveting the parent's "most treasured possession," the parent's spouse! We can suppose that the story is one that Anthony — as well as other children we have met in these pages — might respond to.

While this development of coveting and guilt is normal for all children, it can be very troublesome indeed for some, as we have seen with Anthony and Susie, where it came to interfere with other important matters like schoolwork and sleep.

Severe Judgment Itself as the Culprit

What has become ever more clear to me during my thirty-odd years of intimate exposure to myriad versions of the woes of children — indeed, of patients of all ages — especially in their personal relationships, is this: harsh judgment itself, especially as it becomes the self-accusatory voice of overweening conscience, is revealed to be a culprit under judgment. Indeed, we need only ponder the children's compelling dramatizations of inner torment suffered under the persecuting judge within (Susie's, for example) to see just how demonic this force can become.

If there should be any doubt that the snake in the garden is constituted, at least in part, of severe and unwarranted judgment itself, from without or within or both, let us move for a moment to what can happen within couples' relationships. Think of intimate partnerships you know that are in deep trouble. Then ponder how much of the shipwreck might be caused by each party's experiencing of the other as the epitome and extension of the judging persecutor inside his or her head. A great deal of the work involved in learning to be close to another person is about understanding how all of this kind of misery comes into being and what can be done about it.

Here we might profitably consider for a moment a possible reading of William Blake's phrase "Marriage hearse" in the poem "London." The phrase appears at the end of this famous poem, perhaps more familiar for the opening stanzas, which in themselves are quite congenial with the present subject:

> I wander thro' each charter'd street,
> Near where the charter'd Thames does flow.
> And mark in every face I meet
> Marks of weakness, marks of woe.
>
> In every cry of every Man,
> In every Infant's cry of fear,
> In every voice, in every ban,
> The *mind-forg'd manacles* I hear.[1]

Noting that the poem, in its final stanza, ends with the words "Marriage hearse," I want to explore briefly here the "mind-forg'd manacles" by focusing on marriage itself. In that relationship, and in analogous relationships, there is always the possible death of intimate love by strangulation carried out by the "snake as judgment."

The short version of this frequent painful development is that every in-

---

1. William Blake, "London," in *The Poetry and Prose of William Blake*, ed. D. V. Erdman (New York: Doubleday, 1988), p. 26, emphasis mine.

timate partner is predestined to become a lightning rod for previous versions of feelings of devaluation. Then the rage that always is felt toward the agent that supplements the accusation of the internal judge can be felt especially toward that primary partner. This dynamic, and how it is connected to difficulties in primary relationships, would fill another book if the subject were thoroughly developed. I note it here in order to accent how the devil employs judgment as though it were his own invention and most priceless weapon.

The Bible as Witness?

The most important message of the Bible is not a "moral" one in the usual sense. This point can be clearly seen when we reread that annoying parable of the workers in the vineyard in Matthew 20:1-16. Some worked from early morning, some began three hours later, others started six or nine hours later, and still others began only at the eleventh hour. Yet all received the same pay for their work! Understandably, the ones who worked for the entire day were very unhappy, and they grumbled to the owner of the vineyard. And how did he respond? He spoke not of an arrangement in which each is paid what he deserves as his due. Instead, he spoke of sovereignty over his own graciousness. The point of the story is that the kind of love that the Bible is about cannot in fact be earned. The same message is given by the Psalmist, who wrote, "He does not deal with us according to our sins,/nor repay us according to our iniquities" (Ps. 103:10, NRSV).

There is also the heartening pronouncement in 1 John 3:18-20, which says in effect that, if our conscience, our inner accuser, condemns us, God is greater than our conscience. Here is the suggestion that our judgment of ourselves is itself subject to correction by a higher authority.

And what form does that correction take? We must be clear that the correction of the *demonic* use of judgment does not come through permissiveness. God does not revoke the nature of his righteousness to accommodate human rebellion; but he also does not simply abandon human beings to the "devices and designs of our own hearts," to quote the Book of Common Prayer.[2]

Analogously, in Chapter 4 (pp. 66-68) I emphasized the point that

2. *The Book of Common Prayer*, produced by the Protestant Episcopal Church of the United States of America (New York: Harper's, 1944).

when parental love is not based on this-for-that, we are not at all in the realm of permissiveness. A good parent doesn't simply wash his or her hands of hurtful behavior and abandon a child to impulse. He or she recognizes that the out-of-control child, attempting to act on a destructive impulse, is at the mercy of a force within that he may not be able to withstand alone. Paradoxically, one of those destructive impulses (Susie is a good example of this) is an urge to judge oneself far too harshly. In any event, the parent is there as an ally of that part of the child which is being attacked from within.

Here it is instructive to repeat the quotation from *Hamlet*, at that point near the end of the play when Hamlet is apologizing to Laertes for losing control of himself at Ophelia's grave:

> Hamlet is of the faction that is wrong'd;
> *His madness is poor Hamlet's enemy.*
>
> (5.2.249-50, emphasis mine)

Understanding what it is like to be under siege, the good parent, as well as the good mentor, intervenes powerfully and unconditionally on the side of what is good for the child, standing *with* the child instead of standing *over against* him in judgment. Such a stance is in fact derived from the way that God enters into human suffering with mercy, moving first with grace — not waiting for bad behavior to change — and with patience, that is to say, sustaining and accompanying the human being without coercion.

Susie's Final Word to Us

Susie's remarkable story of crime and punishment illustrated for us the power of parents who are able to *enter into* their child's suffering instead of judging her behavior. At the very end of her work, Susie offered a most remarkable footnote that would seem to speak to the struggle against the snake under the guise of severe conscience. After the repeated jailing and solitary punishment for the criminal in her story, she one day devised a scene in which the policeman had disappeared and could not be found. Since children often represent their own inner monitor as a policeman, it is perhaps not too far-fetched to speculate that this resourceful and creative poetic device may have been behind the report that Susie began to sleep through *some* nights without being waked by the intrusions of her "snake" into her sleep.

The culmination of her drama would seem to suggest that the judgment (the policeman) itself was somehow sensed to be the enemy that had to be rousted. And through her play and through the absence of all judgment by the two maternal figures present, she was able to arrive at the softening, at least, of the persecutory force of her own internal judge.

To end this section, keeping in mind that we are speaking of unwarranted human judgment, we could listen to some memorable words of our poet laureate. Speaking at one point about some of life's richest treasures, she stated simply: "The Judgment perished — too — " (Dickinson, #756).

Summing up Part II and Anticipating Part III

In our guiding poem, Dickinson has given us a lens for looking more deeply into what the three children brought to us in Part I. The series of metaphors she used have provided something close to an outline for this section, beginning with the conception of the implied garden as a way of speaking about the family. Here our focus was on the wells that best nourish the family and on the "beyond deserving" nature of those wells.

Then we took a look at how the role of a parent or of a mentor could be seen as "the minor Circumstance" in that poem, which aptly places parental figures in a secondary, assisting role to the "Major Role" in the drama of the growth of the flower or, by extension, the child.

Now, having developed the metaphor of the snake in the garden that has intruded so monotonously into the human story, and having considered the idea that harsh judgment itself is part of the hidden identity of that snake, we will consider the notion that psychotherapy might be imagined as a new kind of garden. In situations where obtaining one's "right of dew" has not been possible, or where there have simply been more worms than could be opposed, or where there has been too much heat to be "adjusted," or where stinging bees have been too unrelenting, it may be possible to obtain a second chance to ameliorate these adversities that have interfered with the tasks of growing up.

We will finish this chapter, as Dickinson does her poem, with a thought about what we may have learned from the children and others:

To be a Flower, is profound
Responsibility —

III. Remedies and Responsibility Revisited

8. Psychotherapy as a New Kind of Garden

Some readers may find the word "psychotherapy" repellent. Is it not something for weak people who do not take responsibility for their own affairs of heart and mind? Further, has not Sigmund Freud, who is held to be culpable in founding what is now an industry, created a treatment for the few which has become the illness of the many? I will be bold, however, to challenge these objections and to hazard a presentation of what for me have become the essential principles of a process to which I am personally deeply indebted and through which I believe I have been able to be a "minor Circumstance/Assisting in the Bright Affair" of enhancing for some people their capacities for love and work.

In the context of this book, an overview of the essence of psychotherapy, as I understand it, may for some offer an interesting underpinning for what was going on beneath the surface with the children's therapeutic work described in the first three chapters. For others, it may be an excursion into the realm of the unconscious mind through which we might learn something about ourselves, since, as Harry Stack Sullivan so aptly stated: "In most general terms, we are all much more simply human than otherwise, be we happy and successful, contented and detached, miserable and mentally disordered or whatever."[1]

At the same time, I want to be clear that I am not claiming that psychotherapy is right for everyone or that it is the only way to confront the inevitable problems in living that come to all. Nor am I claiming that the

---

1. Harry Stack Sullivan, quoted in Frieda Fromm-Reichmann, *Psychoanalysis and Psychotherapy* (Chicago: University of Chicago Press, 1959), p. 8.

process offers cures, but only a growing ability to struggle better with adverse winds and inner distress and troubles with relationships. Moreover, psychotherapy is not always helpful, and it can be outflanked by opposing forces not vulnerable to its approach.

I will aim for brevity, taking my cue from the patron poet of this book. In one poem she purported to command the very letter she was writing:

> Tell Him — I only said the Syntax —
> And left the Verb and pronoun out —
>
> Dickinson, #494

Such genius for condensation cannot be achieved by ordinary mortals, especially in speaking of the complex subject of psychotherapy, but here is my best effort to condense matters to their essence. If you want the shortest version of all, it was provided by a young patient of mine:

> This is a new recipe; my dolls have not had this before.

What Is This "New Recipe" Called "Psychotherapy"?

First, psychotherapy consists of a special relationship characterized by the qualities of love that constitute the primary subject of this book. It is, in fact, what artists might call an abstraction of the essence of that love into a very specific form. Like a painting, it is bounded very strictly. Like a sculpture, it has its own distinct qualities, limits, and possibilities. Like music, it is a dynamism that operates within the discipline of certain governing principles. And, like a poem, it makes its own way, as Robert Frost pointed out: "Like a piece of ice on a hot stove, the poem must ride on its own melting."[2] All of the arts share all of these qualities, and in all there are techniques that must be mastered in order to practice the art effectively.

I omit here issues involved in psychotherapy as a science, important as those are. These scientific matters are better discussed by experts who work from the scientific angle of vision, especially in the treatment of cer-

2. Quoted from "Robert Frost: The Wisdom of the People," in *Understanding Literature and Life, Part III: Poetry,* audio lecture recording (Chantilly, Va.: The Teaching Co., 1995).

tain organic conditions beyond the scope of my own work. Fundamentally, I understand psychotherapy to be an art.

Who Might Want It?

Here are several examples of likely aspirants for what I am calling a second chance at growing up. There are many who have had insufficient opportunity to pack their own bud of potentiality; who find that something gnaws at their vitals that robs them of love or work; who are thirsty for the elemental dew that was not sufficiently available from well-meaning parents; who live with buried, unadjusted heat that keeps being re-ignited in present relationships; who are frostbitten by winds that were too strong for them; who continue now to re-experience the "goblin Bee — that will not state — its sting," to borrow a few phrases from the previous chapters.

What are, then, the specific form, the limits, and the defining particulars of this art, and the dynamisms that fuel it?

Its Form and Limits

First, the frame and the boundaries. Psychotherapy occurs in a specific place (preferably in the same place consistently), and it is limited to a given time, made clear from the first by the therapist. It is understood to be a professional service for which a fee is charged, the amount of which is agreed upon from the outset.

The contact between the parties is understood to be limited to the sessions and whatever telephone or written communications are appropriate to the therapeutic work. The limits exclude personal or social interchange, either in person or by phone, and except in work with young children, physical contact is precluded. I cannot speak for other kinds of therapies, but all of these limitations are essential to the kind of psychotherapy I practice.

Its Distinct Qualities

How is psychotherapy different from other forms of caring assistance? If much of what happens in sessions is simply "talk," why is it not just as effective to talk over issues with a good friend or a mentor of some other variety?

One of the differences has to do with the fact that the patient employs the therapist as an assistant whose entire role in the relationship is to serve the client. This assistant is not enmeshed in the circumstances of this person's daily living, has no personal stake in what path the client pursues, and is, in effect, a "disinterested" party. Such a stance is of course different from being "uninterested," which would be unthinkable for a psychotherapist.

There is no question of reciprocity between the parties in the focus and subject matter. The session belongs to the patient. As one humorous children's version of the process put it: "The reason the psychiatrist does not mind this is called THE FEE."[3] I hope this is not an accurate statement of all there is to the matter, but it is true that the therapist puts aside his or her own interests and concerns, including his or her own needs for power, in order to serve the client. In any social or personal relationship, this last factor is much more difficult, and probably is not entirely possible to achieve even in the context of which we are speaking.

The task of the therapist is first of all to listen with every fiber of his or her attention to what the client is striving to communicate. This task involves being attentive not only to the surface content of the words spoken, but also, and even more importantly, to the under layer or "bass notes" of the stream of thought as it comes forth. Perhaps most important of all is to comprehend what the client is feeling and to be able to reflect that feeling back with *accurate empathy*. A further task of the therapist is to throw additional light on the drama that unfolds and to do so modestly, always following the client's readiness for more insight and, with rare exceptions, abstaining from advice-giving and problem-solving.

What Are the Dynamisms That Provide Its Potency?

I stated above that this art form shares with music the presence of particular dynamisms that elude our power fully to describe, like Dickinson's thought on beauty:

3. Quoted from Louise Armstrong and W. Darrow, *A Child's Guide to Freud* (New York: Simon & Schuster, 1963).

. . .

Chase it, and it ceases —
Chase it not, and it abides —

Overtake the Creases

In the Meadow — when the Wind
Runs his fingers thro'it —
Deity will see to it
That You never do it —

Dickinson, #516

However, musicians could no doubt tell us some particular requisites of a powerful musical composition, as well as what is necessary for a forceful performance of it. Perhaps this is a loose analogy, but there are also certain given forces operating in effective psychotherapy.

In what I am about to say here, I will no doubt be charged with equating psychotherapy with Freudian psychoanalysis. That assertion is true in that certain aspects of the latter are in my view essential to understanding the power of authentic psychotherapy. I am not speaking of several hours a week on a couch. Most of my work is done in one weekly session, face to face.

However, I must note that in addition to the power inherent in a relationship that transcends a "deserving" paradigm (the major theme of this book), there are specific forces operating underneath an authentic psychotherapeutic relationship that have indeed been made accessible to us through the discoveries of Freud and others after him. These I will touch on briefly.

A Strangely Powerful Dynamism: The Hidden Impulse to Repeat

Although in ever-changing circumstances, old happenings with new cast members in new scenes contribute to our difficulties in growing up, as well as constitute an ongoing "Tooth upon our Peace" (Dickinson, #459), they are an essential component in a second chance at growing up. Without this spontaneous replication, there would be no real access to the springs of motivation for change. We must have the enemies alive in the room in order to address them.

To say that people do the same thing over and over does not at first glance mean very much, and to claim that the entire enterprise of psychotherapy rests on this certainty would seem to many to be absurd.

However, it is amusing to us that Charlie Brown repeatedly subjected himself to Lucy's perfidy. As you will recall, she would ostensibly hold a football for him to kick, only to withdraw it at the critical moment, causing him to fall on his head. After a few replications of this trick, she would lean over his fallen figure and ask, "Are you stupid?" It is funny to us because we ourselves are sometimes drawn into the same traps again and again. How are we to understand this surprising urge to repeat? Here again, the children we met in Part I are our matchless guides.

A memorable example is provided by Henry and his clay sculptures. In session after session he would run eagerly to the plastic bag containing remnants of certain of these sculptures. He would then concentrate his efforts on further demolishing them into finer and finer particles. There was something he was strongly motivated to erase, to annihilate utterly, to remove, perhaps, from his conscious mind altogether. He addressed this matter over and over.

Another vivid example of repetition in the children's play was the way Anthony kept repeating his game of being a bank robber seeking to escape the inevitable retribution he felt he deserved, and struggling with the authorities for dominance.

Children play games again and again to gain mastery over something that the game represents. Every time they repeat a powerful impression, especially in an *active* as opposed to a merely *passive* way, they strengthen the mastery they are looking for. In various forms through centuries and across cultures, the game of "King of the Mountain," for example, has provided children the opportunity to address the same struggle Anthony enacted in his play therapy: the drive for dominance.

In exploring the what, why, and how of children's repetition in their play, Jennie's second visit to the playroom will give us another clue.

In this session Jennie gave the impression that something was being repeated in the playroom that had long been habitual in her daily life. Having been told the previous week that in this place she could choose whatever she wanted to do and say, on this second visit she launched herself immediately into an astonishing, brilliant performance. She had written notes and now displayed by memory a seemingly inexhaustible supply of thoughts, bits of stories, dreams, things she had learned at school, and whatever else came to her as possible ways to excel in her new role. One might guess that all this had something to do to with pleasing this latest authority figure in her life, as well as reassuring herself that she could excel at anything assigned to her, including this new undertaking of psychotherapy.

When Jennie began her work, there was clearly something already going on with her that needed only a new opportunity in order to get resurrected in a new way with a new "other." Freud observed the frequency of this kind of happening, wherein something gets re-enacted rather than consciously thought about or remembered. In speaking of the indestructibility of what lies in the unconscious mind, he spoke of "paths . . . laid down once and for all, which never fall into disuse" and "are only capable of annihilation in the same sense as the ghosts in the underworld of the Odyssey — ghosts which awoke to new life as soon as they tasted blood."[4] Ghosts? We have run across them in earlier chapters. What is it that is apparently indestructible, being resurrected over and over?

Why does a habitual gambler repeat again and again his doomed enterprise, even bringing himself and his entire family to utter destruction, when all probabilities are stacked so heavily against his succeeding? Why does a dangerously obese person continue to eat ice cream or other weight-aggravating foods in quantity, right in the face of medical warnings of illness and possible early death?

This list could be expanded indefinitely. But one excellent example of the point at hand is clear to all psychotherapists, especially those who work with couples: Whatever else goes on in the magnetism between two primary partners, there is inevitably a repetition of something that was at play in an earlier partnership, usually with a parent. There is something unfinished that seems to require a new person with whom to replay an old drama. Very often, if not always, the necessity to reproduce a former play with a new cast is a determinative factor in the selection of the partner, although the persons involved are generally unaware of the nature of this attraction.

This statement catapults us into the matter of a part of the mind that Freud and others felt to be the larger part. They called it "the Unconscious," and they were convinced that this unconscious in some ways plays

---

4. Sigmund Freud, *The Interpretation of Dreams*, standard edition, 5 (London: Hogarth Press, 1900), p. 1.

the major role in our minds. It is one of our mistakes to refer to the unconscious as "the subconscious," implying that it is a minor player.

Repetition: The Immortality of the Unconscious Wish

We will pause over the word "unconscious." Much of what makes life worth living originates in the unconscious mind: the vitality, pith, quick, and spirit of our entire existence. The libidinal currents that make love and pleasure possible, the creativity that finds expression in all art, the vast, unfathomable range of emotional capabilities, and no doubt much more apparently come from this larger part of the mind, the part that lies beyond our awareness. Even the aggression and all the negative feelings that give us so much grief also produce richness of life. Without aggression there would perhaps be no war, but there also would be no sexual aspects or many other important aspects of life.

The matter at hand is how the unconscious mind is involved in the mysterious compulsion to replicate former experience in new guises.

We are back, then, to this question: What lay underneath Jennie's second session and her exhausting performance there? Or, to put it more generally, what is it in all of us that seems to be indestructible and that apparently keeps getting resurrected — as illustrated by the gambler, the obese individual, and the mysterious selection of primary partners — in order to get a second chance at something?

In Freud's view, what is indestructible in the part of the mind that lies outside our awareness is *wishes*. He came to believe through observation that these unconscious wishes are immortal. They will not be denied; they keep on pressing for satisfaction by some means throughout life. If frustrated at the immediate level of fulfillment, these wishes keep seeking other paths of satisfaction, ceaselessly and perpetually regenerating themselves with ever-shifting life situations and relationships.

Further, if not satisfiable directly, the wishes will appear in changed form in symptoms. Indeed, Freud's position was that this part of the mind is capable only of the kind of thinking that produces wishes and all that goes with them, including whatever impulses, weapons of self-protection, and megalomania that further the impetus of the wish for fulfillment.[5]

5. Freud, *The Interpretation of Dreams*, pp. 577-78.

This theory of Freud's is debated. But noting what my child patients accomplished, both in their play and in what clearly got re-enacted with me as their therapist — this new other in their lives — I have come to have considerable respect for it. It provides us with a viable hypothesis about a common source of thorny problems as well as a second chance in life that may be available through psychotherapy.

If the immortality of the wish is what lies under the perpetual necessity to repeat, do we have any clues about the nature of such wishes?

What consistently "rings a bell" with me in observing myself, others to whom I am connected personally, and my patients of all ages is what Freud identified as the urgency to satisfy an infantile megalomaniacal wish.[6] While this common wish has infinite variations in its content and the nature of the attendant impulses, we would all seem to be heirs of some form of it, with its weapons of self-protection and whatever else supports the impetus for the fulfillment of this megalomaniacal wish.

In her therapy with me, Jennie described a dream she had about a pig in her bathtub "so sadly" getting drowned. Later in the same session, she reported that her little sister was "such a pig." This is an excellent illustration of the wish theory. What could the dream refer to other than the threat posed to Jennie's "megalomaniacal" needs of that time by this little sister she sensed as a rival for the supreme place in her parents' eyes?

Notwithstanding our distaste for and our skepticism about the matter of death wishes in the unconscious mind toward loved ones, it appears too often in children's spontaneous play to ignore. Death wishes also appear in our own dreams, but we are generally shielded from confronting them directly through the merciful ability of our dreams to provide disguise. We saw exactly such a wish repeated time after time by little Susie. There was a series in which she arranged the cruel execution of a thinly disguised mother figure, presumably giving an external form to her wish to replace her mother, combined with gaining relief from her own guilt through her own vicarious punishment. By making her mother "the bad guy" who got executed, by identification she could herself "get what she deserved": capital punishment.

Because of the transparency and unguardedness of what children unwittingly reveal in their play, we see with increasing clarity what it is that directs the course of their sessions. Most often it is the power of an uncon-

6. Freud, *The Interpretation of Dreams*, p. 556.

scious wish, along with the threatened consequences of having the wish fulfilled. This combination supplies the urgency and the driving force for the child to find a means, through the toys and materials offered in the playroom, to obtain understanding and relief.

Repetition: A Revealing and Controversial Case

When Marybeth, aged two and a half, was brought to my office, she had for some weeks been experiencing much disturbance in her sleep and was not eating normally. She was irritable and subject to unprecedented temper tantrums and frequent bouts of tears at the slightest frustration. She was unusually fearful and, though previously quite independent, needed to cling to her mother and to be held a great deal.

Marybeth had been an easy, contented baby with a sunny disposition who slept well, ate well, and "was gregarious and outgoing." The troublesome changes seemed to begin shortly after the birth of her little brother when she was sixteen months old.

While strong reactions to the birth of a younger sibling are not unusual, what happened with Marybeth was more serious. I should note that the new baby gave her more than the ordinary load to bear, because he was born with some medical problems involving repeated emergencies and frequent stays in the hospital, necessarily requiring much attention from both parents. A young child no doubt interprets attention as preference, as greater love.

With those developments, Marybeth, a verbally precocious child, began to express and elaborate strikingly on things that were frightening to her, such as worms. More ominously, she reported that the apartment house doorman, who had been a great friend of hers and whom she seemed to like a lot, had threatened "to hit her with a stick."

Marybeth also began to be very preoccupied with the subject of penises. One day she said to her mother, pointing to her belly button, "This is my penis." When her mother explained that her daddy and little brother had penises, but that she and Marybeth were girls and had a different kind of special place, Marybeth was not satisfied. She continued to focus on the theme of penises and said that she had seen Mr. Bob's, a pseudonym here for the doorman. She added that his penis had been "on her bottom."

This announcement understandably alarmed her parents, and they immediately took Marybeth to the pediatrician, who, upon examining her, said there was no visible sign of molestation. But the doctor was also concerned about the child's troubled sleeping and eating patterns, as well as her fearfulness and irritability.

At this point, concern about Marybeth's state of mind as well as what she was saying led to a course of sessions in the play therapy room, where Marybeth, her mother, and I met weekly in order to see what Marybeth's spontaneous, untutored play might reveal.

While much of her play was what all little girls would choose to do with such a plethora of new toys and paints in the supportive presence of two friendly, non-controlling mother figures, it was not long before she discovered a way of playing that took on a marked eagerness and even urgency for her.

What began to fascinate her was what she could do with the homemade play dough, this soft, squeezable substance I mentioned earlier as having been important to a number of children. One day, when she was rolling out the dough and cutting it into shapes with cookie cutters, she said suddenly, "There is a baby in there." She delivered a miniature gingerbread man and presented this "baby" to her mother. Her mother, always a ready responder to the play, accepted the baby graciously, asking, "Is it a boy or a girl?" "It's a dough baby" was Marybeth's noncommittal reply. Within moments, she manipulated the shape a bit and said, "It's a bird now," and shortly afterward, "It's turned into a bear," and then, "Now it's going to go back where it was," at which point she emphatically rolled it back into the dough.

Following this intriguing introduction to a baby that assumed the ability to fly away and also to take on the features of a scary animal, several sessions were spent, with Marybeth's growing excitement, in her insisting on using the scissors to cut up the dough. Cutting it up in this way seemed to be the most important thing in the room for her, and she always returned eagerly to this play as soon as she came into the playroom.

Her cutting up of the pieces of dough began to be increasingly aggressive in its nature, so that her mother and I had constantly to be on guard for her pink fingers, but in vain we attempted to steer her to using the scissors for paper and the kitchen tools for the dough. Whatever Marybeth had in her mind to accomplish with this attack on the dough with the scissors, it began to take on greater and greater importance. One day, after digging furiously for a few moments, she yelled, "I got a fish! I got a fish! Mama, can we cook it for supper and eat it?" Different schools of thought will hear this symbolism in various ways. We will simply see where she went from here.

The fish gave way to the following week's equally spirited excavation, this time yielding a large hunk of cut-off dough, with Marybeth triumphantly announcing, "I got a ball and a pizza!" There would seem to be some intriguing euphony here.

Marybeth still did not seem to be finished with her probe into the mysterious treasures that apparently lay hidden in this dough. The third week she hurriedly ran to her post, took up the scissors, and began even more excitedly to dig in the dough. After some moments of saying nothing, she suddenly cut off a piece of dough from the depths of the lump and cried victoriously, with a big smile and flashing eyes, "I got it! I got it! I got it!" This time she seemed satisfied with her prize, although she did not further identify the "it."

While this enigmatic achievement appeared to be very satisfying to Marybeth, she still did not seem to be finished with the subject. In fact, she began to seem quite troubled and worried about something that did not find a name in the playroom, and her mother reported that she was still unhappy and having trouble staying asleep and was still not eating normally.

Then a new drama began to emerge. Still using the scissors and the dough, but in quite a different mood, Marybeth began cutting off big lumps of dough, dividing them into two pieces, and giving part to her mother and part to me. She then instructed us to try to take the other person's share. Sometimes she gave her mother the larger piece, and then she would change her mind and give me the greater portion. Thoughtfully considering and reconsidering the distribution, she finally arrived at more equal shares, which seemed eventually to settle the matter.

If anyone has missed the secret of what it was that Marybeth pursued so ardently, achieved with such satisfaction, and completed by sharing the treasure between two parties, here is another clue.

At the time of her third birthday, feeling that I was fairly sure what was symbolized by the "ball and pizza" and by the ensuing triumphant excavation, I tried out my theory by giving Marybeth a present of a lovely toy bee with gold silken wings. In an egregious error, I had thought it to be a male bee. Apparently the child knew better: upon opening the gift, she burst into heart-wrenching sobs and wailed, "I want *another* present!" Attempting in vain to comfort her about her disappointment, and thinking perhaps she wanted *more* presents, I learned through her mother's perspicacity that she had wanted a *different* present. She took the bee but left that day unconsoled.

The following week I casually mentioned that there was a little animal in my office that wanted to live where the bee had gone, and would Marybeth be willing to take it home with her? When she unwrapped the tissue paper and found a toy lizard with unmistakably masculine contours, her face lit up with joy and gratitude, and she could not have been more effusive in her appreciation. A thank-you note from her home arrived in my mail that week, Marybeth having dictated to her mother, "I love dorothy. Thank you for my bee and my bug. You are so nice. I want to play again. Love, Marybeth."

It is not so surprising that a little girl would feel keenly a dethronement upon the arrival of a younger brother, and we know that older siblings can indeed experience something like a betrayal on the part of the parents in allowing such a disruptive, inconsiderate intrusion to occur. We can also understand that the brother's special needs, which were taking such a toll on the parents, would add to the expectable feelings of loss on Marybeth's part. She not infrequently made disparaging remarks about this newcomer, saying erroneously, for example, that it was he who had slammed the car door on her finger and caused her injury.

In fact, only the literality and specificity of this accusation were untrue. Marybeth also from time to time stated that she didn't want her little brother to come to the playroom, sometimes making this point emphatically when she was in the midst of her forceful incursions with the scissors into the dough.

The point of this anecdote, however, goes beyond such an expectable reaction of a child to an unwanted rival for her parents' affection. In this instance, the brother's preferential treatment, in her eyes, had become fixed on his possessing a penis, which she apparently sensed as the secret of some special power in her familial situation. Understandably, the unconscious, infantile, megalomaniacal wish for power, to use Freud's term, focused on a wish for a penis. Marybeth expressed this wish by attempting to turn her navel into a penis, by her pronouncement that she had seen Mr. Bob's penis, and by her claim that she had had "a penis touch her bottom."

We have seen that these statements coincided with sleeplessness, a loss of appetite, and unwonted fearfulness, especially evident in Marybeth's saying that Mr. Bob had threatened to hit her with a stick. For most parents, perhaps, all of this would be a signal that somehow this child had been molested. But in fact the doorman had been alone with Marybeth no more than five minutes at a time, and that in a public lobby, when he offered to watch her while her mother got the baby and stroller upstairs. There were, however, enough signs of distress to cause these caring and alert parents to move out of the building immediately. Without a patient exploration of what was actually going on in Marybeth's mind, this situation might well have caused an innocent man to be accused of child molestation, much aggravation of the distress of the child, and even legal entanglements with a wrongly accused party.

Freud discovered the difficulty of distinguishing reports of, and even memories of, sexual child abuse from unconscious wishes. Indeed, the mental health community is still plagued with storms of controversy over claims of "betrayal of the truth" when the possibility of fantasied wish fulfillment is propounded. Certainly it is true that some children are sexually abused, and my story is not meant to dismiss or minimize the importance of preventing such heinous exploitation. However, we need to know that unconscious wish fulfillment is sometimes mistaken for actual fact and can also cause much undeserved suffering.

What became clear through Marybeth's play over many weeks was that this child *wished for* a penis; her casting Mr. Bob in her fantasies was resourceful, in that he was a friendly male figure outside her family around whom the wishes could play. The image of "a penis on her bottom" was simply an extension of her wish to have one appended to her own body. The wish to share her brother's fantasied power was also reflected in her symptoms: she literally wanted to become ill like her brother.

At the same time, Marybeth was experiencing powerful feelings of guilt. Her mind was being tormented by the mixed and troublesome feelings this wish incurred. The anger she felt at the perceived superiority of her brother's standing in the family, and her transparent wish to eliminate this rival altogether, to cause him to go back to where he came from, as she had made her dough-baby do, generated powerful guilt feelings. She was able to mitigate these gnawing feelings of powerlessness, rage, and guilt only by working out a way through her play to share somehow the imagined potency of her brother's penis by repeatedly dividing the prize found in the dough between two parties — her mother and me. She then directed us to grab for, and then gradually relinquish our hold on, the fantasied source of the power until she was satisfied that a just distribution of the advantage had been obtained.

Marybeth's resourceful compromise between the necessity of fulfilling her wish for power by having a penis and, at the same time, the necessity of coming to terms with the demands of the ongoing reality of having to share her parents with her brother was apparently a turning point for her. Gradually her fears seemed to subside, her temper tantrums abated, and her sleeping patterns and her appetite became more normal.

The therapy sessions had to come to an end for reasons of external necessity, and Marybeth was loath to let them go, but she had done enough work on "opposing the worm" of violently conflicting urges to regain her equilibrium. Concurrently, there was an alleviation in other areas of her parents' pressures, including her little brother's health problem, which no doubt contributed substantially to Marybeth's relief. Her simultaneous wish for and fear of her brother's death, which had been sorely amplified by his frequent hospitalizations, were aided by his improving health as well as by her own hard work.

As this story shows, the necessity to repeat is related to the immortality of the unconscious wish: what gets repeated is everything that has to do with the driving force of the wish, including everything not accessible to the conscious mind. In play therapy, all of that is "remembered" mainly through repeating old impulses, attitudes, character traits, symptoms, and weapons of self-protection, including not knowing — that is, remaining unaware of all of these things. We remember Anthony's immortal words: "Fog is important to keep you in the dark."

A Second Powerful Dynamism in Psychotherapy: The Use of the Weapons of Self-Protection

From early childhood, we find various ways to guard our castles from sensed dangers, from inside as well as outside, the inside being largely a matter of our own "wild things," to borrow once more Maurice Sendak's term.[7] Our "wild things" are varied, but many of them represent anger and guilt. These often come from unacceptable wishes, like Susie's transparent

---

7. Maurice Sendak, *Where the Wild Things Are* (New York: HarperCollins, 1964).

wish to replace her mother by repeatedly playing out her execution. The wishes and their retinue of troubled feelings seem to remain radioactive, compelling, and immortal throughout life, ever transforming themselves around new cast members and life situations.

The children themselves have given us charming pictures of some of the protective devices we employ against our wild things, not least this matter of keeping some things out of our awareness by "burying" them. Anthony, while his toy protagonist killed off his enemies, told me, "It is not the end of them; they're going to the bottomless pit." Another time he said, "They buried the bad guys and their stuff underground." When one of the heroes was having "trouble with his gun," he simply threw all the droids into a cave. "The door is underground," Anthony explained. Jennie echoed this idea one day by adding to her jail a second level "where bad guys go when they are *really* bad."

Jennie once used these same words when playing with the animals she created. As she searched for ways to contain her own troublesome feelings, she made stronger and stronger cages for the animals, "where they go when they are really bad."

Some of my child patients who were too old to be interested in my special play dough as symbolic food found a handy use for it as quicksand, in which they could bury their villains.

Actually, this time-honored attempt to remedy gnawing feelings by pushing some matters out of awareness is essential to our sanity. If all of our "wild things" were to thrust themselves into our waking life, we would indeed be undone:

. . . .

What Terror would enthrall the Street
Could Countenance disclose

The Subterranean Freight
The Cellars of the Soul — . . .

Dickinson, #1225

However, this burying approach can be very costly, and that was something the children themselves sensed. More can be buried than angry impulses. Anthony once told me, "When you get knocked out cold, you can't remember things." The reports from school that he was having trouble with "immediate recall" give us a realistic glimpse of one part of the price he was paying for burying his wild feelings.

Jennie had a version of her own. She considered thoughtfully an unruly bus that couldn't be controlled, which she herself overtly said "was very angry," and solved the problem by anchoring the wheels "so that they couldn't move at all." I have seen many a learning problem traceable to just such an attempted solution to impulse: children fixing their mental wheels so that they cannot move at all.

We also resort sometimes to defending our castles by magical thinking, whereby our wishes simply are taken as reality. "My snake is longer than the snake you have here in the playroom," announced one little girl who had a great deal of trouble sorting out facts from wishes. Further considering the stuffed toy she was playing with, she told me, "My snake is more than three feet long — no, even longer; it is as long as this room!" This is reminiscent of a comment Anthony once made: "My brother and I have magic weapons. We can kill each other and then be alive again."

Beyond unhealthy, unrealistic retreats into magical thinking, we sometimes reverse roles in life's drama. Anthony began a session with me by immediately asking me a math question upon entering the room: "Dorothy, how much is four and seven?" Then he quickly cut me off with "Time's up! You failed!" The wish to erase a painful experience simply found a magic solution in the reversal of the cast members of the drama.

This simple reversal of subject and object in our heads is a popular device with adults too. "I'm not angry; you're angry!" We frequently employ this maneuver in our dreams: we place someone else in the role of oppressor and cast ourselves as innocent victim, thus sparing ourselves from looking straight at our own anger or aggression and from feeling the sting of guilt. "Someone tried to run me down last night in my dream." That dream might be traceable to some recent analogous situation of feeling offended by someone in waking life. But it also might be successfully unraveled by interpreting it as an instance of role reversal. Perhaps the dreamer was actually dealing with a recent act or malevolent wish toward someone else. A dream requires interpretation, an interesting joint enterprise involving both patient and therapist that can sometimes play a large role in psychotherapy.

How might the weapons of self-protection come into play in therapy and give someone a second chance to resolve issues? Let us return momentarily to the hidden imperative to repeat old happenings with the cast members in new scenes, and look more closely at how psychotherapy is helped along by this predictable happening. It is true that the stratagems for self-protection described above — stratagems against the gnawing worms and droughts and biting winds and stinging bees — can take a costly toll, necessary as they are. But in psychotherapy these protective stratagems can be played out with a new party, the psychotherapist. Referring to daily life in the outside world, the patient may, for example, describe threatening tensions and battles with others that can occur in personal relationships or in the realm of work. But these *descriptions* will not suffice. In the treatment room itself there has to be a web of flesh and blood to give shape to the enemy forces until they can be brought up from their ghost-like operations in the mind's cellar and revealed in their true colors through interaction with the new other, the psychotherapist. To use different metaphors, the wires have to be hot if one is to see how they need rewiring; it has to be raining for one to detect the leaks in the roof.

Moreover, the struggle between the need to perpetuate the old, familiar ways of taking care of feelings, which, after all, have seniority, and the interloping new force for new and better ways of caring for oneself starts to stir up a war. In the treatment room this potentially healing war takes place outside of conscious awareness; it does not announce itself with trumpets. At the same time, signs of its presence can always be detected by the practiced eye. For example, there is a sudden insufficiency of funds, or time, or both that makes the sessions too inconvenient to continue. Sometimes a patient starts arriving late for sessions or simply "forgets" about them. It occasionally happens that a patient oversleeps, sometimes waking at the very moment a session was to begin.

The usefulness of such a development in making ghosts come alive within a new relationship introduces the third of the powerful dynamisms operative in psychotherapy.

The Third Powerful Dynamism: Dragons, Witches, Fairy Godmothers, and Gods — or, in Prose, "Transference"

A child in therapy might think, "Daddy is a dragon. Now this doctor is a dragon."[8] Or "My mother is a witch. Now this doctor is a witch." Or, to

8. See Armstrong and Darrow, *A Child's Guide to Freud.*

draw on a story we all remember, "This dear grandmother of mine — what has happened to her? I picked her some flowers and brought her a little cake, and she has turned into a wolf!"

And there are other variants on this theme: "I wish my mother were always like this fairy godmother in my book. This therapist lady is a fairy godmother." "This doctor is a magician: she can make all my dreams come true!" "I love this doctor! I would like to be with him all the time!" "I hate this doctor! He is a giant in my attic who roars at me!"

These are a few of the mysterious feelings that can start to attach themselves to any number of helping figures, such as teachers, physicians, pastors, and other kinds of mentors. Some degree of attachment of old feelings to a new helping figure is inevitable, especially to someone seen regularly under the same circumstances over a period of time. In the particular situation described at the beginning of this chapter, the psychotherapist provides a hothouse for these feelings. Here can be found that "web of flesh and blood" so necessary for the old struggles to come to life, in a setting in which they can be re-experienced, brought to consciousness, and revised according to contemporary realities. This web is typically called transference.

Without transference, one of the essential dynamisms for psychotherapy would be missing, although it is not in itself the power. It is what happens within the hothouse provided by the relationship that determines whether a course of psychotherapy will be of life-changing usefulness to the patient. In this context it will be helpful to recall an old story about a man who, apprehended by the law for shooting a bird, said, "Well, I had to shoot that bird. It kept singing about how I had killed my father."

Let us take up first the dragon or the roaring-giant aspect of these feelings, so ingeniously encapsulated in the tale just mentioned. This story accurately reveals what can develop during a course of psychotherapy. At some point the patient may begin to feel as though there is a new giant in his attic who must be silenced. Old, intolerable feelings, such as anger and rage and guilt and powerlessness, can be stirred up against the therapist, making the patient feel that it is necessary to oppose this person who seems to be the instigator of this renewed agitation.

While this opposition is more pronounced in adult work, it can also occur with children. After a few happy sessions with this new grown-up, a child suddenly may not want to attend sessions anymore. Consider that a child who subtly expressed the dark feelings that were starting to arise in

149

her by drawing black borders around a series of pictures of a cat drinking milk from a saucer. Shortly after completing these drawings, the child refused to come anymore, and none of my attempts to reach the child through empathic understanding were effective. It was almost as though the empathic understanding itself was painful to the child, as the empathy stirred old yearnings that could not be satisfied in her real world.

Who would want another round of emotional strains that either were, in the case of adults, present long ago between child and parent, or, in the case of children, still current? Would one want yet another "giant in the attic," or feelings of helplessness relative to a more powerful personage? Would one want a new fear of having one's own signals blotted out by another's, or one's entire life under a new controlling hand?

But a patient may also see this new figure not as a dragon or a witch, but as a warm, uncritical, accepting parent who seems to understand things and is magically going to "solve all my problems." Here the wolf becomes the grandmother, instead of the grandmother turning into a wolf.

It is the task of the psychotherapist to accept all of the feelings that emerge, whether negative or positive, and to use them in the service of the patient. For example, it is here that the giant, the persecutory judgment, inevitably exposes its face, the degree of its severity, and its stratagems to accuse and attack.

One of the most powerful opportunities of the transference relationship is the softening of the severity of this inner attacker, which lies behind much of the suffering in many of the problems in ordinary people's lives. It is often the bane of the schoolchild who "cannot focus," as well as the hidden culprit in marriages that flounder in anger, as each partner increasingly experiences the other as "a bad parent," an amplifier of the internal self-critic in the context of transference. Several of those large tasks of growing up described in previous chapters are fostered by this softening of severe judgment.

The idea of psychotherapy as a new kind of garden where one might have a second chance at those tasks is supported by all of the dynamisms mentioned above.

Insufficient dew from the past may be replenished by new nourishment. Strong winds can be prepared for. As Henry reminded us, "I must not make the rope too short, because if a strong wind came while the boat was anchored, the wind would blow the ship over."

Freedom from the prowling bees of parental correction on the outside and freedom from overweening conscience on the inside can be enhanced. We recall Jennie's intriguing words about the animals she was experimenting with in the playroom: "These animals are very lucky. They can do lots of things — not like the animals that are in captivity."

A good test of the possible usefulness of psychotherapy as a new garden for persons young and old to grow in is that matter of "adjusting the heat." Is such a thing possible? Heat, in the sense of anger, is the big bad wolf that eats at us all, whether or not we are aware of it. In this context we can recall some of the children's versions of this anger as they expressed it in their play therapy.

Anthony, for example, frequently commented on the scenes of violence and annihilation he created. He talked about "a war in outer space," and once vividly described shrapnel that caused "both Pluto and Saturn [in this case, himself and his brother] to be wiped out!" He also made these pronouncements: "The road is burning!" "Purple flames make an obstacle course!" "[I'm] very close to being blind because of the explosion!"

Jennie expressed this anger in different ways, as we observed in her drawings. Once she told me, "The Americans are very angry with the British because of all the bad things they did to them." And Henry gave us this glimpse of his anger when interpreting his drawings of "ugly aliens": "They are terrible. . . . I can't stand to look at them. What if you opened the door, and there they were?"

It is possible to affect positively such angry feelings, to some extent common to us all. Indeed, one of the primary means of doing so is finding in the context of the therapy the capacity to put inner concerns and feelings into words or into the language of play, rather than simply "doing things." Doing something instead of knowing or feeling what we keep hidden from ourselves is one of the central issues addressed by genuine psychotherapy. This is a subject I will discuss in more detail in our next and final chapter.

9. Responsibility Revisited

"To be a flower is profound responsibility." So ends our guiding poem. Does that line hint at a deeper understanding of the meaning of "responsibility"?

In fact, the children we have met in these pages have proved to be our guides about many things, not least about responsibility. We recall Anthony's immortal words, while pouring over a large book as though he were able to read it: "I have to find a way to get out of this mess."

Responsibility Has a History

Respecting Ghosts

With uncanny wisdom, the children knew that the responsibility for their problems did not lie with themselves alone. These problems had antecedents. Jennie's "scary and old-fashioned ghosts" can serve as an encapsulation, not only for the way she sensed the impediments to her own blooming but also for one way all three children took responsibility for what they needed to address in themselves that included a dim sense of an inheritance, something that complicated their tasks of growing up. Anthony mentioned "icebergs that had been there for thousands of years and [were] impossible to thaw out," and in doing so seemed to be referring to something already present before he was born that affected what he had to do for himself. We think of Henry's aversion to ugly creatures he couldn't "stand to look at" that might be just beyond the door. These are evidence of a hidden knowledge in children that, to quote Wordsworth, "fades into the light of common day" in adults.

The children knew that they were not alone in what they were trying to deal with. In Melville's *Moby Dick,* there is a memorable passage in which Ahab talks with the ship's carpenter, who is making a replacement for Ahab's ivory leg. The context is the mysterious continued presence of pain from the crushed leg, so long ago removed. "Hist, then," says Ahab. "How dost thou know that some entire, living, thinking thing may not be invisibly and uninterpenetratingly standing precisely where thou now standest; aye, and standing there in thy spite?"[1]

In *Absalom, Absalom!* Faulkner described the character Quentin Compson in this way: ". . . his very body was an empty hall echoing with sonorous defeated names; he was not a being, an entity, he was a commonwealth. He was a barracks filled with stubborn back-looking ghosts. . . ."[2]

The children we overheard somehow knew about these subterranean spirits that were not of their making, and that knowledge contributed significantly to their being able to take responsibility for their tasks in growing up. They addressed these ghosts as a part of their work.

Taking the Active Role

Anthony's statement in the opening paragraph of this section shows he knew that he had to take the active role in what he needed to do. This same stance was taken by our other two protagonists in their addressing the tasks involved in growing up discussed in previous chapters. In the course of their play, all three children managed intuitively to go about doing things that would pack their buds for future potentialities and help them struggle better with the conflicts that gnawed at them. Their play included symbolic achievement of more of those supplies of the heart, their "right of dew," that contribute to a person's ability to give to others.

Finding ingenious ways to adjust the heat of aggressive and sexual strivings was exhibited by all of the children mentioned in this book.

1. Herman Melville, *Moby Dick* (New York: Penguin, 1992), p. 513.

2. From ABSALOM, ABSALOM! by William Faulkner, copyright 1936 by William Faulkner and renewed 1964 by Estelle Faulkner and Jill Faulkner Summers. Used by permission of Random House, Inc. (New York: Random House, 1972), p. 12.

Strengthening their internal shields against strong winds was exemplified in the covering Jennie devised for her boat, and in Anthony's dramatizing his own weather crisis when his family was being "rained on by computers." We may recall his own assessment: "These people did a crazy thing: they shot a net out over the hole and tried to cross over it. But the suction in the black hole was too strong, and they should have known it was too strong, and it broke the chain."

Modifying the biting stings of severe conscience (escaping "the prowling bee") was perhaps the greatest achievement of all, since it seemed to lead to the alleviation of troublesome symptoms in all of the children discussed at length here. For example, Susie's arriving at the point in her play where the policeman could not be found seemed to signal some relief from her internal persecutor.

Exploring the Cellar, or Making Inquiry

A great deal of what the children did, although they were not consciously aware of it, was to make extended inquiry into hidden dimensions of themselves and the situations they were in. Intuitively addressing and working with what lay beneath the surface, they developed their ability to respond more adequately to the tasks they needed to do, which would seem to be the root meaning of the word we are exploring.

Anthony's inability "to focus and concentrate his efforts" in school gave way to leaping to the 93rd percentile ranking in his performance in mathematics and to the disappearance of any reports that he was unable to attend to his work.

Jennie, in her evolving portrayal of herself through her series of larger and better houses that she created during her play, also appeared to increase her leverage on unconscious forces. Her tic disappeared, as did her difficulties with mathematics and her "spacing out." Her response to the tasks she needed to accomplish in the real world apparently became more able as she successfully addressed the subterranean tasks of her hidden world.

The last boat that Henry made in the playroom, carefully equipped with sails "which would catch the wind and give the ship power," was predictive of the trajectory of his own successful course in the years that followed.

Responsibility and the False Assumption of "Autonomy"

"I am the master of my fate, the captain of my soul"[3] has remained for some who learned the lines in high school a stirring and inspirational thought. It was quoted by Timothy McVeigh, the condemned Oklahoma terrorist, just before his execution. What utter illusion in this person clearly enslaved to the invisible forces working within him! His belief that he had been in charge of himself all along, a free agent making autonomous decisions, is only an extreme case of a very common idea closely related to the popular understanding of "responsibility."

The fact is that the human mind is not made of one piece, fully in control of its actions, able fully to carry out its intentions, acting autonomously on the environment. Although Freud brought this fact to our attention (see the quotation and reference at the end of this section), the point had been made long before Freud by the great minds of antiquity, such as the Greek tragedians. Euripides' *The Bacchae,* for example, is a masterpiece of revelation of the disintegration of human control over its own destiny. Sophocles' *Oedipus Rex* makes clear to us a human blindness in regard to the forces actually in power over the human drama. Shakespeare has the player king in *Hamlet* say,

> Our wills and fates do so contrary run
> That our devices still are overthrown;
> Our thoughts are ours, their ends none of
> our own. . . .

Hamlet, 3.2.1.221-24

Along with our own intentions, regardless of our varying strengths, what we think and will and do, as subjects, is always also under the influence of something else. Whether this "something else" lies solely in the unconscious mind or whether it derives from "God" or some version of "the Devil" will probably never find universal agreement. However, the evidence that human beings are not entirely in charge of their own castles is too clear to be missed. At least it was not missed by Anthony, Jennie, and Henry!

3. William Ernest Henley, "Invictus," in *Modern British Poetry,* ed. Louis Untermeyer (n.p.: n.p., 1920). Poem accessible on Bartleby.com.

Although there are at least two frames of reference announced at the beginning of this book, it may be a bit difficult to be catapulted from the children's work into literature and sometimes theology and current events, and then back into the children's work again. But once again they have something valuable to tell us. We can recall that they generally expressed their sense of this complicated matter by using "bad guys and good guys" in their play. "The bad guys have the horse!" Anthony exclaimed once, as he struggled symbolically with forces seeming to gain power over him.

We adults do not like to face the fact that we are not the sole directors of our thoughts and actions, because it is a blow to our illusion of autonomy and power and pre-eminence in the universe. Freud wrote vividly of this third blow to naive self-conception, as well as the two preceding ones:

> The first [blow] was when they [scientists] learnt that our earth was not the centre of the universe, but only a tiny fragment of a cosmic system of scarcely imaginable vastness. . . . The second blow fell when biological research destroyed man's supposedly privileged place in creation and proved his descent from the animal kingdom and his ineradicable animal nature. . . . But human megalomania will have suffered its third and most wounding blow [from the knowledge that] *the ego is not even master in its own house,* but must content itself with scanty information of what is going on unconsciously in its mind.[4]

Making "Responsibility" More "Responsible"

Given this more realistic understanding of the limitations of human autonomy, what does the word "responsibility" mean?

In this light, responsibility changes its colors. *We are more responsible, not less so, when we are aware of forces that are working on us beyond our ability to control them.* Denial of that truth, along with actions that do not take that truth into account, is the height of *irresponsibility.*

It is a common but curious form of this denial, perhaps having to do with the universal wish to have autonomous power, that underlies a very serious mistake, often under the rubric of "accountability." We often think

---

4. Sigmund Freud, Lecture 18 in *Introductory Lectures on Psycho-Analysis,* standard edition, 16 (London: Hogarth Press, 1963), pp. 284-85, emphasis mine.

that to look for underlying motivations for our own and others' destructive deeds is somehow to "explain away" or condone them, rather than to shed helpful light on them.

In another context, this point is effectively made by Christopher Morse, a prominent theologian of our time. He speaks of the limitations of human "Response-ability." Writing of the misconception that salvation by grace seems to be a confession of human irresponsibility, he argues that, on the contrary, it is grace that enables "the human ability to respond in relationships of love and freedom," which he describes as the ability to respond in "ways that are not imposed against our will and are not destructive of well-being." He thus provides "an alternative reading of responsible freedom and self-determination to that presupposed by theories of autonomous self-sufficiency."[5]

While the context for Professor Morse's statement is different from the one from which we are speaking, his point is actually very helpful for the present context also. Without knowledge of or attention to the "something else" that always influences our choices and decisions, our capacity to respond adequately to what a situation calls for is severely truncated.

Let us leap once more into literature, where Shakespeare in *Julius Caesar* offers us an especially moving example both of the "something else" always at work in human relationship and of the action of love in breaking through to what is needed. At the end of the bitter quarrel between Brutus and Cassius, in the course of which each hurls verbal daggers at the other, a very compelling thing happens as mutual love breaks through the rage:

CASSIUS: Have not you love enough to bear with me,
    When that rash humor which my mother gave me
    Makes me forgetful?
BRUTUS: Yes, Cassius, and from henceforth,
    When you are over-earnest with your Brutus,
    He'll think your mother chides, and leave you so.
                 Julius Caesar, 4.3.121-22

One can say that Cassius is simply making excuses, evading his responsi-

5. Christopher Morse, *Not Every Spirit: A Dogmatics of Christian Disbelief* (Valley Forge, Pa.: Trinity Press International, 1994), pp. 252-53.

bility for his misdeeds by blaming his mother, but there is *power* in the acknowledgment that one brings from his own past some hidden accelerant to a quarrel that makes him more responsible, not less. And Brutus, that "noblest Roman of them all" (5.5.69), however flawed, shows here a level of responsibility not surpassed by that of his public valor. He demonstrates the same quality in his relationship with his servant, Lucius, who keeps falling asleep while trying to play music for his suffering master:

BRUTUS: I should not urge thy duty past thy might;
I know young bloods look for a time of rest. . . .
I will not hold thee long; if I do live,
I will be good to thee.

Julius Caesar, 4.3.260-61, 264-65

To address questions of motivations and forces not visible to the naked eye, both in ourselves and in others, is the very height of responsibility, as it takes into account our limited autonomy. To change scenes once more: What courses of history might have been altered had national leaders had an awareness of unconscious wishes, being thus able to heed Socrates' immortal injunction to "know thyself"? Erik Erikson is said to have posed this intriguing question: What destruction over a century might have been spared the world if Hitler had known about his own needs for power and had perhaps been able to realize his dreams of creation in architecture as an alternative course to destructive aggression?

Similarly, as Barbara Tuchman brilliantly exposes in *The Guns of August*,[6] it was the need for human power that led to the disastrous war of 1914, military plans for which were completed by general staffs of Germany, France, England, and Russia as early as ten years before hostilities began. It is perhaps not widely known that it was the timely reading of Tuchman's book by John F. Kennedy, as well as other members of his administration, that may have changed the course of history in the Cuban crisis of 1962. Apparently pondering how the alarming situation that lay in his hands might be analogous to the immediate precedents of World War I, President Kennedy consciously used the lessons he learned from Tuchman's book to restrain the eagerness of his generals to invade Cuba, possibly avoiding a nuclear war with the Soviet Union. In his book *The Crisis Years*, Michael

6. Barbara Tuchman, *The Guns of August* (New York: Macmillan, 1962).

Beschloss gives us the scene in the Cabinet Room when Kennedy revealed to them that the invasion was not going to happen:

> Admiral Anderson cried, "We have been had!" The Air Force Chief of Staff, General Curtis LeMay, pounded the table: "It's the greatest defeat in our history, Mr. President. . . . *We should invade today!*"[7]

The transparent presence of unconscious wishes for power in these utterances brings to mind the possible presence of unconscious desires for power in the minds of our present leaders in the conflicts in the Middle East. I cannot give this subject the treatment it deserves here, but it is worth pondering in light of what the children we met earlier revealed to us about the desire for power. "Out of the mouths of babes. . . ."

Understanding and Knowing versus Simply "Doing Something": The Great Open Secret of Responsibility

In various instances throughout this book, I have addressed the concept of "acting out." This largely misunderstood idea has come to be nearly synonymous in common parlance with "misbehaving." When children or adolescents are spilling over with unmanageable impulse, for example, they are said to be "acting out."

That expression is better used to refer to keeping subterranean matters from coming to the surface by "doing something" instead of becoming aware of those matters and thereby subjecting oneself to feeling something painful of unpleasant. In other words, "acting out" is a substitute for something else, and that something else consists of two things. The first is to become acquainted with what is happening in one's cellar, so to speak, bringing it to the surface. The second, stemming from the first, is to allow the discernment and judgment of the conscious mind to consider an action before undertaking it.

For example, in the case of a couple in which one party has had an affair, it is virtually always a situation in which the "doing of something" has replaced the knowing and feeling something about the primary relation-

7. Michael R. Beschloss, *The Crisis Years: Kennedy and Khrushchev, 1960-1963* (London: Faber & Faber, 1991).

ship that needs to be surfaced and addressed and worked through. That is an instance of de facto acting out; the term refers to the substitution of *doing* for *knowing* or *feeling* rather than to the "misbehaving" involved.

Most of us know firsthand what it is like to do something instead of feel something. Eating excessively or compulsively, for example, is often used as a way of staying unaware of something uncomfortable that is gnawing at us, and is, unfortunately, successful for a brief time in assuaging a depressive feeling that threatens us. I say "unfortunately" because this is the mechanism that lies underneath the vast majority of cases of tenacious overweight and obesity. The soothing effect of eating something special is very short-lived; bad feelings about the self are aggravated by the attempted solution, because it leads to more weight gain. That is, the attempted antidote to a gnawing feeling then fuels the depression, and a vicious circle is set in motion.

Taking Responsibility for Our Ghosts

Given the immortality of characters living in our own barracks, both the positive characters and the troublesome ones, and given the limited autonomy we have over our actions because of them, how can we be responsible agents in the "love and work" that life is made of?

A part of this responsibility is not only knowing about the positive and negative ghosts that still live within us, but also becoming more aware of their effects on others around us. If we cannot always successfully muzzle one of our negative ghosts, immortally powerful both from genetic inheritances and from environmental forces, we can at least acknowledge its presence, giving voice to the difficulties it may cause others. And at the same time, we can speak of our efforts to struggle against it.

We can then ask, How could a person suffering from depression take this kind of responsibility? While no one suggests that depression can be eliminated by simply willing it away, we can all achieve some awareness that our negative ghosts can severely try the patience of others. Indeed, they can control an entire household, breeding dependency and anger. Simply to acknowledge and give voice to these concerns and to mention one's own efforts to struggle with one's ghosts is an example of exercising responsibility in the context of limited autonomy.

In the microcosm of a single home, one can see the significance of "responsibility" understood in this way. Does it stop there? The kind of love that has been the primary subject of this book has the power to move beyond a particular locus into the world around us and multiply itself — exponentially. Perhaps that fact sheds new light on the mysterious line at the end of Dickinson's poem about love, which we explored earlier:

> Love — is anterior to Life —
> Posterior — to Death —
> Initial of Creation, and
> the Exponent of Earth —
>
> Dickinson, #917

Bibliography

Armstrong, Louise, and W. Darrow. *A Child's Guide to Freud*. London: Faber & Faber, 1963.

Beschloss, Michael R. *The Crisis Years: Kennedy and Krushchev*. Harper-Collins, 1991.

Blake, William. "The Echoing Green," in *The Poetry and Prose of William Blake*, ed. D. V. Erdman. New York: Doubleday, 1988.

Bloom, H. *Shakespeare: The Invention of the Human*. New York: Riverhead, 1988.

Book of Common Prayer. Protestant Episcopal Church of the United States of America. New York: Harper's, 1944.

Dickinson, Emily. *The Complete Poems of Emily Dickinson*, ed. T. H. Johnson. New York: Little, Brown, n.d.

Faulkner, William. *Absalom, Absalom!* New York: Random House, 1972.

———. "Pantaloon in Black." In *Go Down, Moses*. New York: Random House, 1973.

———. Nobel Prize Acceptance Speech. Stockholm, Sweden: The Nobel Foundation, 1950.

———. *Requiem for a Nun*. New York: Vintage, 1975.

Feuerbach, J. *Lieben und Arbeiten*. Available on the Internet.

Fraiberg, Selma. *The Magic Years*. New York: Scribner, 1959.

Freud, Sigmund. *Beyond the Pleasure Principle*. Standard edition, 18. London: Hogarth Press, 1955.

———. *Civilization and Its Discontents*. Standard edition, 21. London: Hogarth Press, 1961.

————. *The Interpretation of Dreams*. Standard edition, 5. London: Hogarth Press, 1900.

————. Lecture 18, in *Introductory Lectures on Psycho-Analysis*. Standard edition, 16. London: Hogarth Press, 1963.

Fromm-Reichmann, Frieda. *Psychoanalysis and Psychotherapy*. Chicago: University of Chicago Press, 1959.

Henley, William Ernest. "Invictus," in *Modern British Poetry*, ed. Louis Untermeyer. N.p.: n.p., 1920. Available on the Internet.

Hölderlin, F. "Patmos," in Friedrich Hölderlin: *Werke, Gedichte* 6, 1850. Available on the Internet.

Jones, T., and H. Schmidt. *The Fantasticks*. Decca, Broadway Original Cast Compact Disk. Chappell, 1960.

Martyn, Dorothy W. *The Man in the Yellow Hat*. Atlanta: Scholars Press, 1992.

Melville, Herman. *Moby Dick*. New York: Penguin, 1992.

Morse, Christopher. *Not Every Spirit: A Dogmatics of Christian Disbelief*. Valley Forge, Pa.: Trinity Press International, 1994.

Robinson, Marilynne. *Housekeeping*. New York: Bantam Books (by arrangement with Farrar, Straus & Giroux), 1981.

Saint-Exupéry, A. *The Little Prince*. English version. New York: Harcourt Brace, 1943.

Scottish Psalter. Edinburgh: The National Bible Society of Scotland, 1911.

Sendak, Maurice. *Where the Wild Things Are*. New York: HarperCollins, 1964.

Tuchman, Barbara. *The Guns of August*. New York: Macmillan, 1962.

Weinstein, A. *Understanding Literature and Life*, Part III: Poetry: "Robert Frost: The Wisdom of the People." Audio lecture recording. Chantilly, Va.: The Teaching Co., 1995.

Winnicott, D. W. *The Maturational Processes and the Facilitating Environment*. New York: International Universities Press, 1965.

Wordsworth, William. "Ode: Intimations of Immortality from Recollections of Early Childhood," in *The Selected Poetry and Prose of Wordsworth*, ed. G. Hartman. New York: Meridian, 1980.

Index

Absalom, Absalom! (Faulkner), 153
Academic achievement, 4, 88-90, 91, 115-16, 146-47
Accountability, 157. *See also* Responsibility of children
Adam (Genesis), 120, 121. *See also* Garden of Eden
ADD (Attention Deficit Disorders), 40-41
"Adjusting the heat," 11-13, 29, 31-32, 54, 56. *See also* Anger; Assisting model; Impulses, control of
Adults. *See* Parents; Therapists
Aggression. *See* Power
Aliens, 51, 151. *See also* Monsters and ghosts; Space wars within play therapy
Amy (case study), 49
Anderson, George W., Jr., 159
Anger: burying approach to, 22; as exaggerated translations of children's hurt feelings, 116-17; guilt and, 51; interferences in work by, 91; represented by scary creatures, 51, 110-11, 116; weapons as self-protection and, 145-46. *See also* "Adjusting the heat"; Impulses, control of
Anthony (case study), 3-24; bed-wetting by, 11-13, 19, 20, 22; burying approach

of, 83, 146; conflicting forces rendered less harmful by, 23; crime and punishment in play of, 71-72; as daydreamer, 4-8, 20; exploring unconscious forces by, 145, 154; external confirmation of improvement, 23-24; guilt of, 123; on false assumptions of autonomy, 156; on past histories, 152; on responsibilities, xxi, 22-23, 152, 153-54; pressure to produce represented by bees, 20-22; repetitive efforts of, 136; robber themes of, 15-18, 136; space wars within play therapy, 12, 19, 61; transference of feelings within psychotherapy, 151; wind in the metaphoric series, 18-20, 113; "work" of, 86
Assisting model: children's need for, 57; controlling vs., 92-96, 112-13; as defense mechanism, 52; in "adjusting the heat," 108-10, 151; interferences in children's work by, 89; overview of, xix, xx-xxi; parents as "bees," 114-19; role of therapists, 134; stick figure model for, 92-93, 113; transference of patient's feelings towards, 148-51. *See also* "Adjusting the heat"; Parents; Therapists
Attention Deficit Disorders, 40-41

Autonomy, false assumptions of, 155-56. *See also* Power

Babies. *See* Infants
The Bacchae (Euripides), 155
"Bad guys." *See* "Good vs. bad guys"
Bank robbers. *See* Robber themes
Barth, Karl, xvii-xviii, 68-69
Bed-wetting, 11-13, 19, 20, 22
Bees, 20-22, 114-19, 154
Beschloss. Michael, 159
"Betrayal of the truth," 144, 155-56
"Beyond deserving" model. *See* Circular exchange model
Biblical sources on love, 78-79, 125-26
Biological framework for child development, xiii-xiv
Blake, William, 63, 78, 101-2, 124
Blame, 121. *See also* Guilt; Inadequacy, perceived sense of
Bloom, Harold, 62
Blooming flowers. *See* Flowers, children as
Boats in play therapy, 50, 54-58, 113
Book of Common Prayer, 125
Books, 109-11. *See also* Fairy tales
Breastfeeding. *See* "Warm breast"
Bribing, 66-68. *See also* Circular exchange model
Buds. *See* "Pack the bud"
Burying approach, 22, 83, 146

Charlie Brown (Peanuts cartoon), 136
Chemical treatments, xiv
Children and child development, overview of approaches to, xiii-xiv. *See also* Infants; Play of children; Psychotherapy
Children as flowering plants, 97-119; addressed by literary sources, 101-3; meaning of for human beings, 83-84; "packing" the bud, 15, 97-100; text of Dickinson poem (1058), xvi-xvii. *See also* "Adjusting the heat"; "Obtaining the right of dew"; "Winds" faced by

children; Assisting model; Bees; Responsibility of children; Snake in the garden; Worms, "opposing"
Christ. *See* Parable of the workers in the vineyard
Circular exchange model, 65-76, 152-61; explained, xiv-xvi; Hosea (prophet) on, 85-86; parental love and, xvii-xviii, 63-64, 68-76, 125-26; for parents, 66-67; punishment based on, 66-68. *See also* Responsibility of children
Computer metaphors, 19-20
Conflicting forces. *See* Impulses, control of; Worms, "opposing"
Control by children. *See* Impulses, control of
Control by parents: "assisting" model vs., 112-13; discipline as, 66-68, 93-94, 112. *See also* Circular exchange model
Coping defenses, 51-53
Cowboys and Indians in play, 8, 9-11, 32
Crime and punishment in play, 71-72
The Crisis Years (Beschloss), 159
Criticism. *See* Judgment
Cuban Missile Crisis, 158-59

Damasio, Antonio R., xiv
Dante, xxii
Daydreamers, 4-8, 20
Death wishes, 14, 71-72, 123, 138-39, 145-46. *See also* Oedipus Rex
Defense mechanisms, 51-53
Descartes' Error (Damasio), xiv
"Deserving." *See* Circular exchange model
Devil. *See* Snake in the garden
"Dew." *See* "Obtaining the right of dew"
Dickinson, Emily: on ability to strengthen oneself (#711), 118; on beauty (#516), 134-35; on bees and stings (#670, 753, 946, 1339, 1683), 114-19; on brevity (#494), 132; on children as flowering plants (#1058), xvi-

xvii, 59. *See also* "Adjusting the heat"; Assisting model; Bees; "Obtaining the right of dew"; Responsibility of children; Snake in the garden; "Winds" faced by children; Worms, "opposing"; on inadequacies (poem 751), 81; on judgment (#751, 756), 122, 127; on love (poems #569, 460, 917, 1411, 1091, 1355), 76-78, 84, 90, 161; on "outside winds" (poem #1656), 111; on private thoughts and feelings (#670, 998, 1225), 48-49, 57, 146; on struggle with impulses (#688, 1046, and 1745), 33, 103; on tight escapes of life (poem #1535), 113; on volcanoes (#175 and 1677), 108, 109; "thief in-gredient" in happiness (letter #359), 121; "Tooth upon our Peace" (#459), 135

Dinosaurs, threats represented by, 5-6, 12

Discipline by parents, 66-68, 93-94, 112. *See also* Circular exchange model

Divine Comedy (Dante), xxii

"Doing something" as responsibility of children, xxii, 151, 159-60. *See also* Responsibility of children

Dominance. *See* Power

Droids, 9. *See also* Star Wars

"The Echoing Green" (Blake), 63

"Eluding the wind" (Dickinson poem). *See* "Winds" faced by children

Empathy, 70, 72-73, 126-27, 134, 150

Erikson, Erik, 158

Euripides, 155

Eve (Genesis), 120, 121. *See also* Garden of Eden

Excessive restraint of children, 93-94. *See also* Discipline by parents

Eye for an eye principle, 65-73. *See also* Justice

Ezekiel (prophet), 82

Fairness, xv. *See also* Circular exchange model

Fairy tales, 81, 109-11, 112, 123

Families. *See* Parents; Sibling rivalry

The Fantasticks (musical), 80

Fathers, 12. *See also* Parents

Faulkner, William, xv, xviii, 23, 82, 153

Fault. *See* Guilt; Inadequacy, perceived sense of

Feelings, transference of, 147, 148-51

Finding and hiding, 6, 99-100

Flowers, children as, 97-119; addressed by literary sources, 101-3; meaning of for human beings, 83-84; "packing" the bud, 15, 97-100; text of Dickinson poem (1058), xvi-xvii. *See also* "Ad-justing the heat"; Assisting model; Bees; "Obtaining the right of dew"; Responsibility of children; Snake in the garden; "Winds" faced by chil-dren; Worms, "opposing"

Fraiburg, Selma, 114

Freedom theme, 34-35, 74, 150. *See also* Impulses, control of

Freudian theory: criticism of, 131; on difficulty of distinguishing reports of sexual abuse, 144; on false assump-tions of autonomy, 155, 156; on im-pulses and restraint, 100-101; on megalomaniacal wishes for power, 143; on repetitive acts, 137; on signifi-cance of children's play, 6, 99-100; on the unconscious, 137-39; psycho-therapeutic relationship to, xxi, 135; references to the Heavens, 79; "to love and to work," 83-84

Frost, Robert, 132

Gardeners. *See* Assisting model; Parents

Garden of Eden. *See* Snake in the gar-den

Genesis, 120, 121. *See also* Biblical sources on love

Ghosts, 152, 160-61. *See also* Monsters and ghosts

Givenness, 69. *See also* Love
God, 79, 125, 126
"Good breast." *See* "Warm breast"
"Good vs. bad guys": cowboys and In-
    dians representational of, 8, 9-11, 32;
    Star Wars, 8-11, 12, 22-23, 151
The Great Train Robbery (film), 15
Guidance. *See* Assisting model
Guilt: anger and, 51; blame and, 121;
    from death wishes, 123, 138; exhibited
    in play therapy, 71-72, 123, 145-46;
    Freudian theory on, 101; sexual
    strivings and, 53-54. *See also* Death
    wishes; Inadequacy, perceived sense
    of; *Oedipus Rex*
The Guns of August (Tuchman), 158-59

Hamlet (Shakespeare), 64, 65, 126, 155
Hands, restraint of, 93
Henry (case study), 40-58; "adjusting
    the heat," 56; boats in play therapy
    of, 50-51, 113; "obtaining the right of
    dew" by, 47-48; on need for private
    thoughts and feelings, 48-49, 57; on
    past histories, 152-53; power sought
    by, 45-46, 49-50; pressures upon, 44-
    45; repetitive efforts of, 136; sexual
    strivings of, 53-54; snails cared for by,
    46-49; transference of feelings within
    psychotherapy, 151; value of play
    therapy illustrated by, 42-44; weap-
    ons in play therapy, 50-52; "winds"
    faced by, 113, 150, 154; "work" of, 87
Hesed, 78
Hidden dimensions of selves. *See* Sub-
    consciousness of children
Hiding and finding in play, 6, 99-100
Hitler, Adolf, 158
Hölderlin, F., 24
Holmes, Oliver Wendell, 35
Honey, 117-18
Hosea (prophet), 78-79, 85-86
Howard Hughes Medical Institute, xiv

Icebergs, 152

Ideological pressures, 112
Impulses, control of: Anthony (case
    study), 23; assisting vs. controlling by
    parents, 93-94, 112-13; children's need
    for, 74; cowboys and Indians repre-
    sentational of, 8, 9-11, 32; direct grati-
    fication and, 89; Freudian theory on,
    100-101; guilt as result of, 101;
    inescapability of, 100-103; Jennie
    (case study), 31; of parents, as result
    of self-doubt, 95; regulated without
    killing, 31-39; self-monitoring capaci-
    ties of children, 117-18; stick figure
    model for, 113. *See also* "Adjusting the
    heat"; Assisting model; Power
Inadequacy, perceived sense of: by chil-
    dren, 6, 38, 53, 116-17, 122; by parents,
    13, 18-20, 81-82, 95. *See also* Guilt;
    Power
Indians vs. cowboys, 8, 9-11, 32
Infants, 66, 98-99, 109. *See also entries
    at children*

"Jack and the Beanstalk," 81, 123
Jennie (case study), 25-39; "adjusting
    the heat" by, 29, 31-32, 108; aggressive
    feelings as Indians vs. cowboys, 32;
    boundaries created by, xxi, 35-39;
    death wishes of, 138; freedom theme
    of, 150; house built by, 27-31, 36-37;
    impulses, control of by, 31, 39, 146-47;
    inner space of, 27-37; on past histo-
    ries, 83, 152; on responsibilities, xxi,
    154; overview of case, 25-27, 38-39;
    playing cards used by, 33-34; repeti-
    tive efforts of, 136-37; self-image of,
    37; sense of nourishment needed by,
    104; snake drawing by, 120; Spot
    (dog), 37, 38; subconscious of, 138,
    154; transference of feelings within
    psychotherapy, 151; "winds" faced by,
    113; "work" of, 87
Jesus Christ. *See* Parable of the workers
    in the vineyard
John (case study), 86

John (NRSV), 119, 125
Judgment, xx, 122, 123-25, 126-27, 154.
  See also Snake in the garden
Julius Caesar (Shakespeare), 157-58
Jung, Carl, 62
Justice, xv, 14, 64, 72. *See also* Circular
  exchange model; Law of the talion;
  Retribution

Kandell, Eric, xiii-xiv
Keats, John, xv
Kennedy, John F., 158-59

Law of the talion, 65-73. *See also* Justice
LeMay, Curtis, 159
The Little Prince (Saint-Exupéry), 98,
  110, 113
"London" (Blake), 124
Love: Bible on, 125-26; children's need
  for, 90-91; circular exchange model
  and, xvii-xviii, 63-64, 68-76, 125-26;
  definitions of, xv, 84-86; psychotherapy and, 132; qualities of, xvii-xviii,
  68-76, 161; sources of, 76-79; work
  and, 90-91
Lucy (Peanuts cartoon), 136

The Magic Years (Fraiburg), 114
Manipulation, 66-68, 74-76. *See also*
  Circular exchange model
Marriage, 62, 124-25. *See also* Parents
Marybeth (case study), 140-45
Matthew (New Testament). *See* Parable
  of the workers in the vineyard
McVeigh, Timothy, 155
Megalomaniacal wishes for power, 139-
  43, 156. *See also* Power
Melville, Herman, xx, 82-83, 103, 153
Mercy, 69-73, 79, 126. *See also* Patience
Merit, xv. *See also* Circular exchange
  model
Milton, John, 120
Moby Dick (Melville), 82-83, 103, 153
Monsters and ghosts, 38, 116, 137, 152-53.
  See also Aliens

Mothers. *See* "Warm breast"; Parents
Motivations, 33, 157-58
Murderous feelings towards parents, 14,
  71-72, 123, 138-39, 145-46. *See also*
  Oedipus Rex

Neuroscience, xiii-xiv
Newborns. *See* Infants
Nourishment. *See* "Obtaining the right
  of dew"

"Obtaining the right of dew"
  (Dickinson poem), 12-13, 24, 47-48,
  57, 70-71, 104-7. *See also* Responsibil-
  ity of children
"Ode: Intimations of Immortality from
  Recollections of Early Childhood"
  (Wordsworth), 65-66, 87
Oedipus Rex (Sophocles), 13-18, 121, 155.
  See also Death wishes
Old Testament. *See* Biblical sources on
  love
"Opposing the worm" (Dickinson
  poem). *See* Worms
Original sin, xx. *See also* Snake in the
  garden
Outer space, 8-11, 12, 19, 22-23, 151

"Pack the bud," 15, 97-100
Parable of the workers in the vineyard,
  xiv-xv, 79, 125
Paradise Lost (Milton), 120
Parental love. *See* Love
Parents, 61-79; as bees. *See* Bees; empathy of, 70, 72-73, 126-27, 134, 150; fathers, 12; general observations on
  family, 61-63; inadequacy, perceived
  sense of by, 13, 18-20, 81-82, 95; as the
  "main garden," xvii-xviii; as "minor
  Circumstance," xviii-xix; mothers.
  See "Warm breast"; murderous feelings towards, 14, 71-72, 123, 138-39,
  145-46. *See also Oedipus Rex;* past experiences of, xviii-xix, 13, 69, 82-83,
  152-54, 160-61; redefinition of family

Index

and, 63; winds affecting, 111-12. *See also* Assisting model; Marriage
Participation as quality of love, 69-73
Past experiences of parents, xviii-xix, 13, 69, 82-83, 152-54, 160-61
Patience, 73-76, 126. *See also* Mercy
Paul (New Testament), 79
Peanuts cartoon, 136
Play dough in play therapy, 141-43
Playing cards, 33-34
Play of children, xv, xvi, 42-44, 86-90, 99-100, 136-45. *See also* Psychotherapy; *specific cases by child's name*; Therapists
Pluto. *See* Outer space
Poetry of play, xv-xvi, xxi
Policemen, judgment represented by, 126-27, 154
Power: children's drive for, 45-46, 49-50, 110-13, 118-19, 136, 156-59; counter forces to, 51-53; megalomaniacal wishes for, 139-43, 156; perceived loss of, 7; ships as metaphors for, 54-58. *See also* Impulses, control of; Inadequacy, perceived sense of
Preoccupations. *See* Spacing out; Work of children
Preschoolers, 99. *See also entries at children*
Private thoughts and feelings (poem #670), 48-49, 57, 146
"Profound Responsibility" of children. *See* Responsibility of children
Psalms, 125
Psychotherapy: ability of parents to enter into suffering of children via, 72-73; "adjusting the heat" within, 151; causes of termination of, 148; defined, 132-33; empathy of therapists, 150; form and limits of, 133; Freudian theory and, xxi, 135; overview of, xiv, xx-xxi, 131-51; patients of, 133; qualities of, 132, 133-34; research trends in, xiii-xiv; role of therapists, 43-44, 148, 150; therapists as "medical droids," 9;

22-23; transference of patient's feelings towards therapists, 148-51. *See also* Assisting model; Play of children
Punishment. *See* Discipline by parents

Reading to children, 109-11, 115-16. *See also* Fairy tales
Reciprocal exchange model. *See* Circular exchange model
Recognition, children's need for, 6
Religious pressures, 112
Remorse. *See* Guilt
Repetition in play, 135-45
Requiem for a Nun (Faulkner), 82
Rescues. *See* Hiding and finding in play
Responsibility of children: active role of, 89, 98-100; Anthony (case study), 22-23; "assisting" role in, defined, xix; within children themselves, 80; "doing something" and, xxii, 151, 159-60; essence of, xxii; false assumptions of autonomy and, 155-56; making more "responsible," 156-59; past histories and, xxi-xxii, 152-54, 160-61. *See also* Assisting model; Circular exchange model
Retribution. *See* Justice
Reward. *See* Bribing; Circular exchange model
"Right of dew." *See* "Obtaining the right of dew"
Rivalry within families, 21-22
Robber themes, 15-18, 121, 123, 136
Robinson, Marilynne, 62

Saint-Exupéry, Antoine de. *See The Little Prince*
Scary creatures, 38, 110-11, 116, 137, 152-53
School. *See* Academic achievement
The Scottish Psalter, 78
Self-criticism. *See* Inadequacy, perceived sense of
Self-monitoring capacities. *See* Impulses, control of

Self-protection, 145-48

Sendak, Maurice, 109-10, 145-46

Sexual abuse, reports of, 140-41, 144

Sexuality of children: bees representational of, 114-19; connotations of snake in the garden, 120-21; guilt and, 53-54; *Oedipus Rex* (Sophocles), 13-18, 121, 155

Shakespeare, William: on false assumptions of autonomy, 155, 157-58; on justice idea of reward, 64; on love, 65, 85; on struggle with impulses, 103, 126

Ships in play therapy, 50, 54-58, 113

Shogun, 12

Sibling rivalry, 21-22

Size, perceived insufficiency in. *See* Power

Snails, care for, 46-49

Snake in the garden, xix-xx, 120-27

Socialization, 115

Socrates, 158

Soldiers, 151

Sonnet #18 (Shakespeare), 85

Sonnet #19 (Shakespeare), 103

Sophocles. *See Oedipus Rex*

Space wars within play therapy. *See* Aliens; Outer space

Spacing out. *See* Daydreamers

"Splat" (Anthony's story), 9, 12

Star Wars, 8-11, 12, 22-23, 151

Steinbeck, John, 15

Stick figure model for assistance, 92-93, 113

Strength. *See* Power

Subconsciousness of children, xxi, xxii, 38, 122-23, 137-45, 154

Submarines, 55-58. *See also* Ships in play therapy

Suffering. *See* Empathy

Sullivan, Harry Stack, 131

Sun. *See* Outer space

Susie (case study), 70-73, 122-23, 126-27, 138, 145, 154

Talk therapy. *See* Psychotherapy

Tender vs. excessive restraint, 93

Tension cells of Anthony, 9

Therapists: empathy of, 150; as "medical droids," 9, 22-23; role of, 43-44, 148, 150; transference of patient's feelings towards, 148-51. *See also* Assisting model; Play of children; Psychotherapy

Thief themes, 15-18, 121, 123, 136

"The Three Little Pigs," 110-11, 112

Toddlers, 99. *See also entries at children*

Transference of feelings, 147, 148-51

Truth, betrayal of, 144, 155-56

Tuchman, Barbara, 158-59

Unconscious obstacles to growth. *See* Subconsciousness of children

Volcanoes, 108, 109

"Warm breast," 70-71, 104-7. *See also* "Obtaining the right of dew"

Water, love as source of, 119

Weapons in play therapy, 50-52, 56, 145-48

Where the Wild Things Are (Sendak), 109-10, 145-46

William (case study), 91, 105-6

"Winds" faced by children, 18-20, 55, 110-13, 150, 154

Winnicott, D. W., 98

Wordsworth, William, 65-66, 87, 102, 153

Work of children, xix, 86-91, 99

World War I, 158

World War II, 158

Worms, "opposing," 7-8, 13-18, 27, 100-103